Next time off a crow Crows don"!

I'M NOT THE MANAGER HERE

A Memoir

And they are hell bent on revenge !!

LINDSAY RAE BROWN

Contents

	Copyrights	VI
	Author's Note	VII
	Dedication	VIII
1.	Part 1: Sylvan Lake	1
2.	One	3
3.	Two	7
4.	Three	10
5.	Four	14
6.	Five	18
7.	Six	21
8.	Seven	26
9.	Eight	30
10.	Nine	32
11.	Ten	37
12.	Eleven	40
13.	Twelve	43

14.	Thirteen	49
15.	Fourteen	53
16.	Fifteen	58
17.	Part 2: Red Deer	61
18.	Sixteen	62
19.	Seventeen	66
20.	Eighteen	71
21.	Part 3: Victoria	75
22.	Nineteen	76
23.	Twenty	81
24.	Twenty-One	84
25.	Twenty-Two	88
26.	Twenty-Three	91
27.	Part Four: Sylvan Lake...Again	97
28.	Twenty-Four	98
29.	Twenty-Five	102
30.	Twenty-Six	104
31.	Twenty-Seven	107
32.	Twenty-Eight	111
33.	Twenty-Nine	115
34.	Thirty	119
35.	Thirty-One	122
36.	Part 5: Lethbridge	125
37.	Thirty-Two	126
38.	Thirty-Three	128
39.	Thirty-Four	131

40.	Thirty-Five	135
41.	Thirty-Six	139
42.	Thirty-Seven	142
43.	Thirty-Eight	146
44.	Thirty-Nine	150
45.	Forty	153
46.	Forty-One	156
47.	Forty-Two	159
48.	Forty-Three	163
49.	Forty-Four	167
50.	Forty-Five	170
51.	Forty-Six	175
52.	Forty-Seven	178
53.	Forty-Eight	180
54.	Forty-Nine	183
55.	Fifty	186
56.	Fifty-One	189
57.	Fifty-Two	191
58.	Fifty-Three	194
59.	Fifty-Four	200
60.	Fifty-Five	203
61.	Fifty-Six	207
62.	Fifty-Seven	210
	Afterword	213
	Acknowledgements	217
	About the Author	219

Copyright © 2024 by Lindsay Rae Brown

All rights reserved.

No portion of this book may be reproduced in any form without written permission from the author except as permitted by Canadian copyright law.

Book Cover by Lindsay Rae Brown

ISBN 978-1-7382836-0-6

First edition 2024

Author's Note

When I set out to write a book three years ago, it occurred to me that I already had one. Arbitrary pieces of paper shoved into desk drawers, random diary entries scribbled haphazardly into notebooks, and countless online articles all had one glaring theme—my love-hate relationship with the world of work.

This isn't to say the challenging task of crafting a memoir was done. Creating a cohesive work that makes sense of the absurd and often half-cocked memories of the past is daunting. With helpful early feedback from some wonderful friends and my dedicated editor keeping me on track throughout the process, I managed to pen the story you are about to read.

The narratives within are true and written to the best of my memory, although some are portrayed in a satirical fashion. Some dialogue between characters has been devised to add depth or clarity to specific scenes. Well, except for the *Catapillar Boy* chapter. That conversation was word for word because not even the wilds of my imagination could conjure that up. Some names and places have been changed to protect the privacy of those I continue to drag into these tales.

To Jamie,
The best (and sexiest) teammate I've ever had the pleasure of doing business with.

Part 1: Sylvan Lake

One

As a seven-year-old, I was afraid of everything. I'd watch my dad fill up his tires at the gas station and worry that he wouldn't know when to stop the air. I worried the tire would explode in his face and leave him horrifically disfigured. Birds of any kind scared the bejeezus out of me. Their beady little eyes and jerky movements were the stuff of nightmares. I constantly needed affirmations of love from friends and family, afraid they had turned on me overnight.

There is one thing I am not afraid of—hard work. I have Dad to thank for that. Dan Sawyer and I can rap about work for hours. From the time I was small and marching around the house in my mom's oversized shoulder-padded blazers and singing cabaret at the top of my lungs, he knew he needed to find some common ground. That was when he brainwashed me to think that the most crucial thing in life was working hard.

When I was seven, my family and I moved to a rented acreage just outside a tiny Albertan hamlet called Markerville. At that time in my life, potion concocting was my favourite pastime. A derelict wooden table stood just off Mom's enormous garden. Here she'd pot flowers or mix the proper sandy soil for her pepper plants. She was always at this table doing something, but not today. Today the table was all mine.

Various Tupperware containers were scattered across the table's surface and each held a whimsical brew. A mixture of muddy water and dandelion petals glimmered in the sunlight. Bright red poppy blossoms filled another of my miniature cauldrons. Many were half-filled with lotions pilfered from Mom's bathroom cabinet. I planned to infuse these with the stinging nettle plants I had carefully plucked from the ground the day before.

Just as I was pulling on a pair of bright yellow rubber gloves—essential safety gear for any intelligent nettle handler—I looked up to find Dad's round face staring down at me, with his usual somber glare. I willed him to walk away. I was too deep into it now. I couldn't very well stop; the gloves were already on.

"You can't just play all day, Linds," he said, reading my mind. "We've got to get the spuds into the cellar."

The cellar was, by far, the least magical place on Earth. My potion table was filled with colourful treasures that held endless possibilities. There I could create fantastical concoctions that could make all my dreams come true. Whereas the cellar was gloomy and smelled weird. It held few possibilities other than death by boredom. Mom always told me I wasn't allowed to go down there because if the potatoes went bad, I could pass out and die. Yet here Dad was, tearing me away from my nettle lotion and forcing me into a pit full of poisonous potatoes.

That's the problem with being small—you're always getting crammed into tight spaces. It was my job to stand under the tiny cellar window, directly inside the potato bin. As Dad poured the tarp-load of spuds through the window, I arranged them tidily into the bin. To motivate me, Dad talked through the window, saying things like, "You doing okay down there, Linds?" and, "Hope the Boogie Man doesn't want any taters right now, or he might gobble up one of your toes!"

Despite his encouragement, I was still afraid. The cellar's only light hung in the middle of the room and gave off about a foot of dim light in each direction. Of course, the potato bin was placed in the far corner of the pit that we called a basement, so the dangly light's reach came nowhere close.

"Dad?" I asked. "Dad?" No answer. *Great*, I thought, *he was out there having a smoke break while I nearly peed on the potatoes out of the genuine fear that the boogie man was lurking in one of the other three dark corners of the room.*

That's when I heard a low growl, "Fe Fi Fo Furl I smell the toes of a little girl!" and a lumbering figure came hobbling toward me from the rickety steps leading down from the kitchen.

Cute, Dad. Real fucking cute.

Finally, the chore was done. I was permanently scarred and would do everything in my power to never enter a dirt-floored cellar again, but this was not something I understood then. Seven-year-old me was only concerned with my lotions and potions and concocting an elaborate plan to convince Dad that he needed some nettle moisturizer on his face.

"Hey, Lester," Dad said, using his long-standing nickname for me. "Come have a beer before you get back to your stuff." We headed to his workshop, where a cold Canadian waited for him, and I found a dusty, forgotten pick-a-pop lodged in the back of the shop fridge. I sat down on one of Dad's rusty chairs while he lit a smoke, and we cracked our tin can tabs in unison.

"I know you don't like doing these chores, Linds," he began, with a severe look on his face. "But it's important you know how to work, kiddo."

"I know," I said because that seemed like the response he was looking for.

"I see way too many useless kids these days. And not to mention their lazy parents. They don't know how to lift a finger for the things they want. You never know what life'll throw at ya, but if you're willing to put an effort out and do the work, you'll always be ahead of the game."

I nodded my head in agreement, hoping this gesture hid the blank stare I was giving him. I was seven! I didn't care about hard work. I cared about my damn potions.

This state of affairs would go on for years. Me trying to get out of work, and my dad lecturing me for being too lazy. From stockpiling enormous logs from the forest for our wood-burning stove every fall to raking our extremely long gravel driveway because I was dragging my feet in the pebbles on my walk to the bus, there was never a shortage of menial labour to keep me busy as a child.

In the years to come, I'd convince so many people that picking rocks from a field is a fun summer pastime that it's no surprise my surname is Sawyer.

Two

Digging through countless bins of soiled tablecloths is the perfect time to identify one's mental health problems. There's something about scraping what looks like a smooshed chocolate brownie (but may very well be regurgitated wedding cake) out of fine linens that really makes a person think about their life choices.

My mental health problems are the same as when I was seven. I am afraid of everyone and everything that crosses my path.

I'm afraid to try anything new. Afraid to put myself out there. Afraid of all the strangers I might have to speak to if my husband decides to drag me along to another work function. I'm afraid of how at ease I feel cleaning mystery crust off hundreds of black round-top chair covers.

I work for an event rental company. The work is pure. A cascade of dirty laundry flows into our warehouse daily, and it is my job to clean it. I have an industrial-sized washing machine and all the necessary detergents to do my job adequately. I have a giant ironing press to ensure a wrinkle-free product. I have a bagger and sealer to finish the job off. I am a professional launderer.

That's my day job, at least. The one I do for a steady paycheck, so people will get off my damn back and stop asking me, "So, what do you do all day?"

My passion is writing jokes, but as any hopeful creative knows, earning a living off your dreams is a long shot. So I've built a resume of mid-level, customer service jobs. My "art" is cleaning up other people's messes.

To anyone peering through the tiny windows nestled in the large bay door of the warehouse, I resemble a lowly laundry wench. There I am, hunched over a stained satin overlay, delicately dabbing a concoction of rubbing alcohol and Super Clean cleansing solution in a circular motion so as not to ruin the elegant fabric. I'm sobbing, blubbering even, because none of the eighteen-year-olds who work here will assist me in my scrubbing. Also, these kids are no good at scrubbing, so the task falls solely on my stooped, age-spotted shoulders.

My hope is that the secret solution to remove stains from satin is embedded deep within my salty tears. This thought makes me cry harder, and I pray my plight will be resolved soon. But I am much more than the wench this silent spectator sees before him. I am a mother. A writer. A humour-lady. A woman. But most importantly, in this place, I am a chemist. I have spent hours mixing concoctions at random, hoping to find the one solution that will solve my woes of stainage in this laundry hellscape. There is a creative element that comes along with devising stain removal potions. The glee of embarking on a puzzle that needs solving is a bewitching prospect that I've been chasing my entire life.

David, my boss, cringes each time I say, "I think I'll do some scrubbing today," because he doesn't know what will become of his precious warehouse and the stock within it. But oh, how lucky am I to have a boss like David. David is a diamond in the rough when it comes to employers in the 21st century.

David knows I am a sensitive soul and need constant praise and accolades to maintain my cheery working disposition. In this knowledge, he remains a cut above the rest. In many places of employment, titles mean everything. You work to attain the title. Once you have the title, you become rich with power and lord that power over the tiny peons below you. You may even lose sight of the work because the power has gone to your head. "My precious," you whisper as you stroke that little plaque on your new office door that haughtily reads *Manager*. Meanwhile, all those below you scramble to usurp your position so they can covet the all-encompassing manager's role.

David has all but eradicated this hierarchical business model. Yes, we have department heads called managers, but it's made clear that no one is more important than anyone else. Each cog in the machine is there for a purpose, and unlike many business owners, David is there beside us, maintaining the cogs to ensure we are happily turning out products.

When I scrub in my warehouse, I scrub with abandon. Jugs of cleaners surround my table, and I pour and mix at random. Eventually, something will take out this stain. Of that, I'm sure. It's just a matter of getting there. Yet, in the hope of "getting there," I risk blowing up the building with some unfortunate mixture I didn't realize was combustive. That, or I will concoct a sleeping potion that will asphyxiate all those who surround my scrubbing station. Scrubbing is dangerous work.

Regardless, the laundry room is a place of peaceful solace for me. A home away from home where I can problem solve, and craft potions and use my imagination without judgment. There I allow my deepest darkest fears to wash away down a drainpipe to who-knows-where.

Three

Some kids entered into entrepreneurship with lemonade stands. My first business was in the softcore porn industry.

Mom never liked crowds. She never revelled in big parties, and our once-a-year trip to the mall for Christmas shopping always ended abruptly and without warning. After about an hour in that hellscape of packed-tight human bodies, she'd throw her hands in the air and proclaim, "That's it! I'm done. I gotta get the hell outta here."

So, when it came to getting new clothes, our family's motto was "To the Sears catalogue!" The Sears catalogue is the great grandmother of Amazon. It would be cringing into its doilies with the barrage of alpaca print panties and sexy Nick Cage pillows we are bombarded with online today.

I remember a particularly badass pair of faux snakeskin pants I ordered that made me feel rad, like I was finally a put-together woman. I'd pair those bad boys with my black pleather jacket and ironic Big Bird shirt, and there was no stopping the suave awesomeness exuding off me.

My deep dive into porn-slinging was before all of this, though. Who knows, maybe these first escapades into self-employment gave me the confidence to rock ill-fitting snakeskin pants and become the very cool person that tens of people on the internet have come to hesitantly love.

The Sears catalogue does, however, hold a direct connection to how I began my porn swindling business. As Mom and I flipped through the thick magazine, I desperately tried not to give myself a papercut on the shiny thin pages. Mom took extra care while passing by the ladies' underwear section to look for sales, but it was my brother Dustin who caught my eye when I noticed how spellbound he was by this portion of the magazine.

This gives me an idea, my little brain stump mused. I hatched a plan as I brushed my teeth that evening. I could make a fortune selling the ladies' underwear section to the boys at school who hadn't yet found their dad's porn stash. Of course, this business would never work these days, considering I googled "Fisty Cuffs" the other day and got a plethora of images of fists up to the cuffs (down to the cuffs?) in random people's assholes. It is essential to know how to spell, kids. Stay in school.

Creeping out to the kitchen in the dead of night was easy. Mom and Dad were always in bed early, and their room was on the other side of the house. Finding the illicit materials was more challenging because the Sears catalogue is enormous. After flipping madly for several minutes, I located my soon-to-be money maker. The only sound in the kitchen, besides my heavy breathing, was the refrigerator's hum. Also, the nervous sweat beads that rolled from my forehead and plunked onto the linoleum floor. Although I knew that what I was about to do was a crime, I couldn't pinpoint the charge. Ripping up Mom's favourite magazine was bad, but ripping it up to sell to my dewy-eyed classmates seemed even worse. I knew what I was doing was wrong. But it felt so good. I then made the ace move of attempting to tear out all ten pages of the lingerie section at once. The ruckus was reminiscent of a sonic boom. Still, my parents did not wake from their slumber.

Clambering up the school bus stairs the following day, I wore an evil grin. I had a whole week ahead of me and a knapsack stuffed with steamy pics of nut huts and honker hankies. I had decided it was rather unfeminist of me only to sell the women's underwear pics, so I found the men's section and tore those hunks out too. To this day, I fully stand for objectifying ripped abs and rock-hard butts only if we do so equally among the sexes.

My first lesson in self-employment? Distribution is difficult. Like, really difficult. Once the word got out that there were half-naked adults in my back pocket, everyone wanted a piece. I was selling my goods for twenty-five cents a pop, and the demand was weighing me down. I enlisted a few friends to help. That's when I learned my second lesson in business. Don't trust anyone but yourself. Those assholes were giving out freebies to cute boys! Gah, did I have to do everything around here?

It turned out I did. No employee will ever be as invested in your business as much as you are—business lesson #3. Lesson #4? Word of mouth is king. This is a truth that I've learned repeatedly ever since my first delve into the world of self-employment, and I don't think that it will ever get old. People will talk if you have a good product with fair prices, and that talk spreads faster than Miss. Piggy when Kermit busts out his banjo.

The schoolyard was aflutter over Lindsay and her backpack of baddies. I had set up shop in a clandestine corner of the jungle gym, hidden away from disciplinary eyes. I laid my merch on the pebbled ground and allowed the clients to choose their goods. I had just as many girls as boys purchasing my naked pages, which proves that all kids are pretty curious when it comes down to it. Get out of here with your boys will be boys bullshit. Then, lesson number five hit me without warning, and it hit me hard. Crime Doesn't Pay. As I looked up at the gangly red-headed boy currently rifling through my stack of naughty knickers, I saw something much more dire. Three teachers, arms crossed, stood directly beyond the jungle gym's outskirts. They were not impressed with my budding entrepreneurial skills.

The twenty-plus pictures I had doled out to various children during morning recess were confiscated and, I assume, locked away in some permanent file with a sticky note on the front saying, "This bitch is going to be trouble for us in her later years." I can't remember the severity of my punishment, so honestly, it couldn't have been that bad, right? I do remember that they never took the money I had already earned. I spent that cash on a grape flavoured Slurpee. It was the sweetest damn Slurpee I've ever tasted.

So actually, I guess crime does pay. As I sipped my grape slushie, I thought about other creative ways I might be able to score a little cash in my free time.

Four

I was never much of a babysitter. Living on a farm in the middle of nowhere provided little opportunity to make money watching the nonexistent neighbour kids. Maybe I could have procured a few gigs here and there from family friends with small children, but I was never asked.

"There's just something about that girl," I imagined the adults in my life saying over their dinner-time conversations. "She's not evil, but definitely not the kind of kid we want to look after our little darlings."

For, you see, I was indeed strange. At the age of twelve, I decapitated all of my Barbie dolls, shaved their plastic scalps with my mom's pink Lady Bic razor, and hung their craniums from my bedroom roof. I wasn't trying to be outlandish or attention-grabbing. I just wanted a different theme than what was previously considered normal pre-teen decor.

For this reason, my life as a babysitter was finished before it had even begun.

Except for one time. The summer following my thirteenth birthday, a friend of my dad's asked if I'd like to babysit his children so he and his wife could go on a much-needed date. This man hadn't seen my bedroom art. I accepted the offer, and before I knew it, Dad was dropping me off at their remote mansion-cabin in the woods. These people were loaded.

A log cabin connoisseur must have drawn up the blueprints for this monstrosity of a home. Created for the kind of person who wanted the quaint feeling of country life combined with the wannabe luxury of the one percent, colossal log pillars framed the front of the house. Massive gardens surrounded the property, and a four-car garage was stuffed with too many quads and dirt bikes to count.

I was able to get a glimpse inside before entering the home through an enormous bay window looking in on the living room. There, neatly placed on a shelving unit, were all the high-tech gizmos one might expect from an abode like this.

Sky-scraping pines surrounded the back porch and there in the middle of the deck was a high-end hot tub. Young and good-looking, my new employers offered me all the iced tea and potato chips I might want for the next several hours while they were out. *If this is what babysitting is all about, count me in,* I thought. Then I met the kids.

The little girl—I'll call her Gracie—was sweet with a glint of *I'm-going-ruin-you* in her eye. I introduced myself and held out my hand to give her a high five just as she booted me in the shin and screamed, "I don't want some fatty babysitting me!"

"Oh, don't mind her," the mother said. "She's just going through a phase."

One or two years older, the boy came stomping down the stairs, and I smiled while rubbing my now throbbing leg. I will call the boy LSD, which stands for Little Shit Disturber. The name is fitting not only because he did disturb all the shit, but he also gave me the feeling that I was on some sort of hallucinogenic trip. The pure havoc this child created out of thin air was the stuff of nightmares. Horrible, terrifying, drug-induced nightmares.

As the two children stared up at me, the parents left, and I wondered what we should do. "So, are you guys hungry?" I asked, falling back on my knowledge that human beings tend to enjoy eating food.

"Uh yeah, stupid," LSD said. "Make us dinner."

I made macaroni and cheese from the box, and we enjoyed our meal on the picnic table beside the hot tub nestled into the patio's deck.

"So, tell me about the hot tub. Do you guys use it often?" I asked, trying to make pleasant conversation.

"Mommy and Daddy have sex in it," Gracie said.

"Ah, I see," I said, trying to match her nonchalance. "So what's your favourite subject in school?"

"It's summer holidays, idiot," LSD piped up.

Since any topic brought us back to some awkward (for me) conclusion, I suggested watching a movie.

As I was getting the VHS player loaded, LSD shot me in the back of the head with his Nerf Gun. It was a huge bolt-action thing and it terrified me.

"What the fuck, dude?!" I yelped. I immediately regretted my use of language.

"Strike one," the boy replied snottily. "Three strikes and my mom will never use you again for babysitting." The way he spit the words at me made me understand that the child had employed this method with previous sitters. He was an expert in the ways of being babysat, and I, nothing but a novice, must bow down before him.

I made popcorn, and the three of us sat down to watch *Homeward Bound*, an epic tale of a cat and two dogs venturing across America in hopes of finding their lost owners. I didn't realize how into the movie I was until Gracie yelled, "You're getting popcorn all over Mom's couch. She's going to be so mad!" Then LSD shot me directly in the eyeball with his bolt action rifle from a distance of about two inches.

"Fuck," I cried upon impact. And LSD whispered the words *strike two* menacingly in my ear.

The parents had told me that their little angels didn't require a bedtime on weekends, so we could stay up late watching movies. And that's precisely what we did. Eventually, LSD laid down his gun and fell asleep with both Gracie and me on the massive sofa.

If a creepy stranger had watched us through the window, they would have smiled at the picture-perfect scene of us snuggled in tightly. That is until I peed on the kids.

I was no bed-wetter, even as a small child. So why now? Why, in this place of splendour, would my bladder decide to let flow? Was it the fear of getting shot in the face again? Perhaps it was gallons of iced tea I'd been drinking during the movie. Either way, somewhere along the line, there had been an accident.

I tried to slip off the couch without waking the children, but Gracie had fallen asleep directly on top of me. My efforts were for naught.

"Gross," LSD groggily shouted. "Did you pee the couch?"

"No," I replied a little too fast. "I think," I fumbled for an explanation but was hard-pressed to find one. "I think Gracie might have had an accident." I gestured to the girl's pants groping for some evidence to my claim. It was at that moment I heard the front door being unlocked.

"Mom!" LSD screamed, "that stupid babysitter you got us just pissed all over the couch and Gracie!"

The mom looked at me. I looked at the mom. My face, red and guilty. Her face, a mix of bafflement and disgust, unable to comprehend the situation she had walked into.

"I, uh," I stammered, "I think Gracie had an accident." It was all I could bring myself to say.

"Oh no, not the couch!" The suede couch soaked in urine was the mom's number one priority.

LSD's dad drove me home. We rode in uncomfortable silence while the smell of urine wafted between us. Upon dropping me at my front door, he handed me three ten-dollar bills. He did not invite me to "babysit anytime" as, I assume, so many date-night-hopeful parents do.

I spent my hard-earned cash on a few fancy notebooks and a ton of candy. While sucking down my Starburst sweets, I wrote about my recent humiliation in my new diary. I had done my time as a babysitter and was now back to the drawing board when it came to potential money-making schemes.

Five

Carlee is filling a large plastic bag with small plastic bags. It's taking an incredibly long time. I've been working with Carlee in the laundry room for almost a year. We make our schedule based on the various events and activities in our lives. Which is to say, the hours we work end up being pretty random. Why David is always praising our hard work is honestly beyond me because we are the least reliable team members on his payroll right now.

Before Carlee, I was a regular employee who followed a regular schedule made by my employer. Working at Lethbridge Event Rentals felt more like a job back then. Nowadays, it feels like home. Well, home with a dash of therapist's office thrown in, because if there's one thing Carlee and I know how to do, it's unpack emotional baggage.

Like, right now, for example, the static in the air is causing Carlee's blonde hair to stand on end. Her tiny frame is moving frantically as she tries to locate and grab all of the plastic bag-ends that need collecting from the floor and saved for later use. She's shoving them into this larger bag-end that should be able to hold them all. Meanwhile she's animatedly recounting the multiple problems she is facing in her everyday life.

Carlee is so cool compared to me. She's outgoing and uber-confident in everything she says. She's studying to be a nurse, and she's well-travelled. She's got two adorable girls. She's always out doing something. Whether it's being a bridesmaid in one of her many friends' weddings, volunteering at her kids' school, or, I dunno, accepting the Most Wonderful Human Ever Award, Carlee is the epitome of put-together. Even when complaining about her problems, she's still laughing and cool about it.

When we were randomly teamed up for a laundry shift a year ago, I immediately cleaved onto her, like a bedbug to an unsuspecting purse. I started surreptitiously hinting that we should, uh, maybe plan our shifts together, and bless the good lord, Carlee agreed. Within days of that first meeting, we had spoken to David and explained that we were going to start coming in for evening shifts together. Carlee needed to work around her classes, and I was now unwilling to work with anyone but Carlee.

Carlee is still talking about life and the chaoticness of it all, and she's still shoving clear plastic bag-ends into the larger bag-end bag. It occurs to me that something strange is afoot.

What sort of magic is this? Have we discovered a black hole bag that might be able to hold infinite bags? What the hell is going on? She's been filling this goddamn bag for hours—or at least ten minutes.

Carlee notices me looking at her and the multitude of bags surrounding her. She is suspended in a sea of thin plastic sacks—a polyethylene princess. Yet the bag she has been shoving all the other bags into remains empty. Bone dry of bags. I can tell by the confusion in her eyes that she, too, is now realizing how long she's been collecting the bags on the floor. She stops what she's doing, takes stock of her situation, and calculates the quandary. Meanwhile, a small robot voice is chiming on repeat through my head, "Does not compute."

Her face blooms from rosy pink to red. Rather than finding a bag to hold all the loose bags, she grabbed a plastic sleeve of a thing (a bottomless bag). There she is, shoving bags madly into this *bag,* and without either of us noticing, they were falling gracefully out the other end of the sleeve, back onto the floor, where she picks them up for the umpteenth time to shove in the top of the sleeve again. Comedy perfection.

When working in a laundry room, almost everything takes teamwork. Folding large tablecloths, bagging, then sealing the linen bags and putting them away in the enormous warehouse, most of it is much easier when you've got another set of hands to help. But everyone folds, organizes and laughs in different ways.

Except for Carlee and me. Maybe it's from our many shifts together, but we seem to be twinning in the way we do our job. A few weeks earlier, I was forced to work with a new laundry partner as Carlee was sick with a flu bug. This new girl was okay. She was a good worker and took the little direction I gave her. There were a lot of awkward silences, and then at one point, probably because she could sense that all I was thinking about was my ill-lost laundry love, she asked if Carlee and I were sisters.

"Ha!" I said because Carlee and I look nothing alike. If Carlee were a majestic gazelle, I'd be that weird cow-pig my kid recently crafted out of a hunk of clay in art class—all lumpy and shiny with no discernable facial features. Rough around the edges, to be sure.

I advised my coworker that, no, we weren't related. Afterwards as I thought about it, I realized why she might think so. It's the cackling. Oh how we cackle. There we are, Carlee and I, wearing our casual laundry wench badges, working so fast in our tiny laundry room that if someone were to videotape us and speed up the footage even half a second faster, we'd resemble one of those fast-action loop vids of people who can do really cool stuff at an incredible pace—you know, those ones you see on Facebook all the time.

We rarely lull in conversation topics and can be heard cackling loudly throughout the warehouse. We have synergy. Carlee's unabashed confidence pairs well with my penchant for strong female leads.

Six

I moved to Sylvan Lake with my family when I turned eight. Before that, my memories are a blur of random solitary moments that do not fit together in any rational way. Probably because being a kid is very similar to being blackout drunk. You know that shit was happening around you, but you're too busy having fun, puking, or crying hysterically to remember anything.

Sylvan Lake was where my real life began. It would be the place I'd make many of my lifelong friends. Similarly, there I'd meet the enemies I still loathe to this day. I'd learn how to drink and smoke cigarettes while playing truth or dare in small playgrounds until the cops would break up our midnight shenanigans. Sylvan, as we called it—because using the word lake each time seemed monotonous and world-weary—would be my home for the next fifteen-some years. I'd grow to both hate and love that strange little town.

Sylvan Lake's main attraction for teens was the pier that juts out from the main street and onto the expansive lake. It wasn't a rickety wooden structure that swayed to and fro when a gust of wind picked up. Instead, it was a solid thing.

On any given summer day, a gaggle of my fourteen-year-old friends and I could be found wandering indiscriminately about the pier. Like freshly beheaded chickens, we'd roam aimlessly. With the distinct odour of marijuana smoke wafting around us, slathered in suntan oil, we'd bellow to middle-aged men from the pier's edge, asking if they'd take us for a ride on their boat. We'd be sassy to the officers policing the beachfront, steal bystanders' sea-doo keys, and throw them high into the pine trees' upper branches to drive home how jerky we could be.

We didn't know how much danger we were in, how these actions could land us in some real trouble because, as is the case with all rowdy teens, our brains were no longer in control of our bodies. We were bikini-clad hooligans, smoking cigarettes and drinking Big Bears, hidden in the shadows of the towering pine trees. Our teenage audacity was showing, and no one could tell us anything.

Train tracks ran directly from the back of my family's rented acreage into the town of Sylvan. On any given weekend, I could be found walking the tracks into town to meet up with my friends. There was always the possible risk of having to jump into the ditch if you heard the familiar whistle of the train and the curmudgeonly engineers screaming, "Get off the damn tracks!" as they passed you by in their locomotives.

A small bridge made from rotting wood marked the halfway point from my place out in the middle of nowhere to all my friends' much more accessible homes located within Sylvan Lake. This is the price you must pay for having rural-loving 'rents who love the smell of fresh country air. Fresh country air?! Really? Try enjoying the fresh country air when your social life becomes nonexistent because you don't have a ride into town on a Friday night, Dad!

Trying to explain these very important conversation points with my parents was a lost cause though, so that's why I began trekking into town on the train tracks every weekend. I was meeting my best friend, Janelle, at the ancient, rotted bridge on one such day, dangling my feet over the edge and smoking pot out of a discarded beer can gleaned from the ditch below.

"Fancy meeting you here," Janelle yelled as she approached from the gravel road.

We were always saying things like this. "Occupied," I'd importantly howl whenever she'd knock on the bathroom door while I was taking a poop. Janelle was the sister I never had, the person to whom I could tell every single one of my secrets. She was also the one who most frequently met me at the bridge. That was evidence of her superior friendship.

Once at the pier, we'd chat and laugh and gossip about our absent friends and push each other into frigid green waters. I was just about to throw myself into the water, showing off my exceptional swimming skills, when I remembered I needed to call home to check in with Mom. Since this was before cell phones, I wrangled up the energy to hike the five minutes to A&W and the closest payphone.

"Hey Mama, sorry I'm late calling," I said while eyeing a suspicious, gooey white substance on the side of the receiver.

"Well, it's a good thing you did call. A woman named Sheri just phoned and wanted to bring you in for an interview." Her voice was chiding. "Anytime this afternoon is fine, she said."

"Awesome! I think that calls for L-Y-N-D-Z-E...." I had concluded a few months prior that the regular spelling of my name was too commonplace, so I came up with this jazzier spelling and was using it obsessively to try to get it to catch on. It never did, aside from my little circle. My "little circle" being solely me.

Upon hearing my self-proclaimed cheerleading, Mom cut me off. "Okay, just get over there. It's about time you get a job."

"Yep, will do, Mother Dearest!" The storm clouds moved in as I ran across the street and back to the pier.

Sylvan was not a big town, so it was only about a seven-minute walk to the fast food eatery where my prospective new career awaited. Perhaps I would have missed the rain if I hadn't taken the time to brag about my new job position. Maybe if I hadn't foolishly taken those extra few moments to puff from the communal joint, I wouldn't have had to task my friends with the unfortunate job of wrestling me down to stick drops in my eyes, all the while screaming mixed messages at them like, "DO IT! DISREGARD MY FLAILING!" "You're killing me. I can feel the liquid hitting my brain!" and, "I can't show up with bloodshot eyes!"

As soon as I set off, the downpour hit with full force. By the time I reached the doors of the infamous fried chicken haunt, I caught a glimpse of myself in the reflection of the large restaurant windows.

There stood a girl in a jean miniskirt. The mascara she'd layered on that morning with practised ease now ran mournfully down her cheeks. Her hair was Pennywise-scarlet due to a lousy dye job the week before. She likened her long multicoloured scarf to a personal amulet—never to be taken off despite the sweltering heat. The scarf was now sodden with rainwater and hanging from her neck like a noose.

Despite all this, I pressed on. Maybe I had a good feeling about this place. Maybe it was just a raging case of teenage arrogance.

"Hi, there!" I said to the woman behind the cash register. She had one of the kindest smiles I'd ever seen.

"Hi," she said and held out her hand to shake mine. "You must be Lindsay."

My interview with the manager, Sheri, was less intimidating and more like a couple of old friends meeting for the first time. We talked about my dishevelled appearance, and she told me there had been more than one time she, too, had been caught in the rain. She showed me around the restaurant as if I'd already got the job.

After an hour of coffee and chatting, Sheri told me she'd love for me to work there. I was a little bit flabbergasted because the interview wasn't an interview at all. At least not one that I'd ever imagined. She gave me some starting paperwork to fill out at home and bring back the following weekend when I'd have my first training shift.

I thought, *'Wow if all interviews are like this, I'll never have a problem getting a job.'* It turned out I wouldn't need to look for another job for some time. I worked at that place until I was eighteen years old. There I'd meet my future husband Jamie, although we wouldn't go on to date seriously and get married until years later.

I'd experience some of the best and worst times in that place. I learned responsibility and accountability. I learned how to work as a part of a team. Even though that team teased me relentlessly most of the time, I'd come to love all my coworkers like family. At my first job as a fried chicken slinger, I learned to understand why work is so vital to the human experience. Coming from two very hard-working parents, I'd always had a strong work ethic, but maintaining a job at the young age of fourteen helped secure a commitment to work for the rest of my life.

Seven

Canada Day was always the money ticket for great days in Sylvan Lake. Drunken tourists packed the streets. They had journeyed to our legendary town for lake living and beachfront bar hopping. By midday, Sylvan would be so packed that merely walking seven minutes from work to the pier took over twenty.

On this particular Canada Day, I aggressively threw elbows to reach my intended destination while cradling a tub of chicken under my left arm. I was in a sour mood. Some dickwad had been hassling me at the restaurant earlier that day. He was adamant that we take the chicken he had purchased, but instead of packing it in the designated stamped paper bag, this guy wanted us to put it in the freezer for a while.

I was on my way to the freezer, goods in hand because, hey man, I don't care how you like your chicken, when my supervisor intercepted me.

"What do you think you're doing?" she asked as I cleared a barrel-of-chicken-sized spot in the walk-in freezer.

"This dude wants his food frozen for some reason. Stupid tourists." I wish we had had some neat towny line that we used for tourists, like OOTers (out-of-towners), but we weren't that clever.

"Oh no, you can't do that." Her face shrunk into a frown. "That's against all kinds of food regulations," she told me.

Why I decided to use that moment to argue is still beyond me. Why didn't I say okay and move on with my day? Perhaps it was my argumentative nature surfacing, or maybe I wanted this dude to get his frozen chicken. Who can be sure now, so many years later?

"But we put cooked food back into the fridge at home. What's the difference?"

"I don't care what you do at home, Lindsay. It's not done here. You'll have to tell this guy no."

"I'm sorry, I just really don't understand why this is a big deal?" I said, holding firm in my frozen chicken position.

"If you're not going to tell this customer no and deal with your other customers, then I'll have to. And then I'll have to ask you to leave because you're not doing your job."

So, it came down to this: warm chicken or bust.

I begrudgingly carried the still-hot bucket of chicken toward the front service counter, bracing myself for the multitude of anticipatory chicken eaters. As I reached my cash register, it was a madhouse. I envisioned a literal chicken coop, but instead of chickens, it was humans clucking and pecking one another. A revolting scene. How could a person stand in this type of shoulder-to-shoulder line, cramped with strange bodies, breathing air already in somebody else's lungs, just for a measly bucket of chicken? Gah, people are the worst.

"I'm so sorry, sir," I said to the man now impatiently waiting at my register, "but my supervisor has advised me that we are unable to freeze this chicken for you due to food safety concerns." I delivered this information with a huge shit-eating grin on my face. In retrospect, this may have only caused more vexation toward the situation.

"That's the schtupidest thing I ever heard! What's wrong with you people?" he said with a heavily slurred accent.

"Again, I'm so sorry, sir. But if I could move along this transaction, I'm sure you can see I have a very long line of hungry people to serve." Once more, my chipper demeanour and unwillingness to sympathize with this man were not helping our current situation.

"Fuckin' bitch," he said, glaring directly into my soul while the smell of beer wafted off his breath.

I then jumped the counter, flung myself onto his back, and slammed him to the floor with my ninja skills. I told him that his name-calling and rudeness were unacceptable and would not be tolerated in this place of business. All while holding him down in a chokehold and giving him a nuggie. Then the surrounding patrons body-surfed me back to my station at the register while cheering me on and gushing over how pretty I was.

No. I only wish that had happened. Instead, I rolled my eyes, placed his bucket of chicken on the counter to my left, and asked who was next in line. The guy abandoned his pail of thighs and keels and went screaming out of the store, calling me all the names in all the books. I was far too busy to care.

I was too busy to care until I wasn't busy anymore. Then, I was done with my shift, and I cared a great deal. Who did that guy think he was? Why am I to blame for this fine establishment's impeccable health codes and food safety standards?

At least I'd got a free chicken dinner out of the deal. Sure it had been sitting on the counter for the last two-and-a-half hours, and that's why my supervisor kindly offered it to me rather than trying to salvage it for another order, but my friends wouldn't mind. I'd be the hero of Canada Day, showing up with room temperature chicken for all.

Now, if only I could get my hands on something to drink. I'm sure I could find someone adequately sozzled in this crowd of drunkards to boot for me, but the problem was I didn't have any money. Why did I spend my last twenty-three dollars on that lime green halter top that had the dimensions of a bandanna?

Nearing the pier, I grabbed a chicken leg and tossed it to a nearby rogue child. *The wildlings.* His hair was matted, his face soiled with red-rock dust from the beach's walking paths. I knew if I didn't give up a piece willingly, he'd attempt to fight me for it. Catching the fowl fodder between his teeth, he started panhandling down the beach by doing backflips for the passing tourists.

I found my besties, Ashley and Janelle, once reaching the pier, and they immediately went for the chicken. See, you can buy people's love with fried food. As we ventured to where everyone was sitting, Ashley nearly tripped over a body lying on the ground. I figured we should probably check if it was alive and, if not, call an authority. A dead body would surely kill the town's celebratory buzz. Upon further investigation, I discovered it was Frozen Chicken Dude. Wasted and passed out on a grassy knoll behind a garbage can.

"This guy!" I screamed, pointing at the man, now unconscious on the ground. "This guy was a total jerk to me at work today!"

"Well, let's throw him in the lake," Janelle said matter-of-factly.

"*Yesssss,*" I mused as I stared into the distance and rubbed my hands together maniacally. Janelle was always the brains of the operation. Looking back, I fear I may have been the evil one.

"I'm kidding, you loser," she said.

"Pfft, yeah, me too," I replied disappointedly.

"But we could jack that bottle of booze he has in his pocket."

"No!" Ashley, our excruciatingly kind-hearted friend, said. "We can't do that, you guys."

"He called me a bitch because I wouldn't freeze his chicken." My two friends stared at me blankly.

"Is...is that some kind of sexual thing?" they asked.

While explaining that chicken freezing was in no way related to sexual acts, I cautiously reached into this stranger's cargo pockets and slipped out the mickey of whiskey. It didn't go far between seven teenagers and the fact that we had to pour one out for our dead homies, but that didn't matter. I was victorious, and that's what truly mattered. I believe it may have been this moment that shaped me into the individual I am today. Well, shit.

Eight

When I smell laundry sewage, I think of Carlee. That's because drains run under the warehouse floor, and sometimes they get a bit stinky with all the machines running. It's always Carlee who cleans the drains. She does this because she inherently understands I'm too apathetic to do anything about the smell. Sure I can muster some giddy-up over the things I love, like laundry work and writing and reading nonsensical comment threads on Twitter for six hours straight. But when it comes to something so tedious as a smelly drain, I will simply put up with the stench rather than do any extra work to remedy it.

Every time, Carlee takes it upon herself to clean out the drains with a concoction of water, vinegar, bounce sheets and various other odour busters. It's a wonder we haven't blown that place up yet. Regardless, each time I see Carlee filling up the little blue bucket with her magical drain cleaning concoction I think to myself, *I am so lucky to have such a thoughtful and intelligent work pal. I hope things never ever change.*

I don't want to be dramatic, but on a cold February morning, out of nowhere, Carlee admitted she was leaving me. Okay, it wasn't out of nowhere, per se. I knew she was finishing up her nursing degree, and there was a small section of my brain that kept whispering, "She's not going to work here forever. She's going to leave because now, with this fancy nursing diploma, she's going to have to go yank weird things out of people's butts and shave acres of pubic hair for pre-op surgeries." Listen, I don't actually know what nurses do. I'm sure it's way more important than that. But I was upset, and my brain goes to weird places when I'm sad.

"Hey, so I know someone who would love to take over my position," Carlee texts me one morning shortly after breaking up with me.

Hmmm, this seems suspect, I think while reading the text but having no plans to reply to it. Carlee knows that I won't reply. Replying would mean setting a universal change in motion and although I'm not adverse to all change, my work wife leaving me is not the sort of change I'm open to. Carlee understands at her core how much I hate the kind of change that I have nothing to do with. So instead, she presses on without waiting for a reply from me.

"My mom, Susie! Seriously, you'll love her. She's just like me!"

Nine

The old gag, "The word gullible is written on the ceiling," has been known to work on me more than once. In succession. Within minutes of the last proclamation. I guess it's because I want to believe in my fellow human. I want to see the good in people and not have to be wary of all those who cross my path. I want to have faith in something other than myself.

I am not a dummy (it just took me three times to figure out how to spell dummy), but I am gullible. Usually, I can see what's coming when people tell me a joke-lie. I know something's fishy when one of my kids tells me there was a zombie sighting in South Korea because as far as I know, zombies haven't been invented yet. Or there was that one time Dude said the party was a mandatory no-pants party. The logical part of my brain says, *Maybe I should question this.*

Except a more significant, louder part of my brain screams, *let's see how this plays out.* Zombies in South Korea? Now that would shake things up a bit. My naivete was never more evident than when I was working in the fast food industry. The number of times I was duped into replacing the walk-in cooler air by capturing it into large garbage bags and releasing those bags into the dining room was countless. I sifted the pre-sifted flour for hours on end because that's what was being asked of me. I even fell for the classic prank of leaving my street clothes accessible to my coworkers and finding them as rock-hard ice blocks after my shift from spending the past eight hours in the freezer.

I'M NOT THE MANAGER HERE

One of my supervisors at the fried chicken store was named Dylan, and he was the meanest and simultaneously hippest grade twelver I had ever met. At the time, I was a measly grade nine loser, and I was surprised he even spoke to me. I don't know what Dylan's reputation was at school, but he was the too-cool-for-fried-chicken guy at work. Do you know who Dylan was? He was Jim from The Office but at a chicken factory. Dylan was always pulling pranks but never got in trouble because the manager loved him. He was always finding creative ways to get out of doing his work and charming all the customers with his witty commentary. Dylan was just there, always in the spotlight because people were drawn to him.

I can't remember a time when Dylan wasn't teasing me—this, however, is not a Jim and Pam story. It's more of a Jim and Kelly tale. I'm Kelly, the vapid, self-centred and, yes, gullible girl whom Jim begrudgingly befriends because I've given him no other choice. Dylan would poke fun at the way I'd have to climb the stock room shelves to reach the 20 oz cups or how I could barely see over my till because I am vertically challenged. Once, I was scheduled as his runner while he was on cash. When I arrived for my shift, I found two phonebooks stacked neatly on the floor where I was to stand behind the pop machine.

"What's this?" I asked.

"Oh, I just thought you might need an extra boost to reach the pop machine while working today," Dylan said, rolling his eyes into the camera.

But I used those phone books with pride. It was nice to see over the machine and into the sea of patrons while I worked. So, who knows, maybe Dylan *was* looking out for me. Probably not, since every time a new customer approached his till, he said, "Hello and welcome." He'd motion to his right where I stood, "This is Lindsay, our greasy chicken dwarf." And because I've always been a bit of a showboater, I immediately loved the attention and gave the customers some jazz hands and a little jig. Almost everyone loved it. They were charmed by the rag-tag team at the Sylvan Lake chicken dispensary, which kept them coming back for more. At least, that's what I'd like to think. It was more likely the sodium-rich, deep-fried batter that kept them coming back for more.

One stormy afternoon I was working with Dylan on cash, and I noted how large the waves crashing onto the lakefront were. The restaurant had enormous windows lining the front of the dining area and looked directly out onto our town's expansive lake—the money maker, as nobody called it.

"Holy man, it's really storming out there. I hope there isn't a tornado!" I said, worry creeping into my voice.

This gave Dylan his opening. "Well, it's not tornadoes you have to worry about. It's the hurricane."

"Hmmm, that doesn't seem right. I don't think hurricanes happen on lakes," I said cautiously. Dylan was more intelligent than me, so maybe he was onto something.

"Suit yourself. I don't care if you believe me. But I did hear on the radio that there's a hurricane watch for Sylvan."

"What? Seriously?" I screamed. "Well, what do we do if a hurricane happens? We'd get demolished being this close to the lake." The familiar heart-hammer of an overstressed brain began to drum in my chest.

"That's exactly the problem," Dylan said. "So, we'll need to get on the roof as soon as possible. Once the wave comes, it'll crash through those windows, and then we'll drown in here. The roof is our safest bet."

"Oh no!" I said, genuinely alarmed.

"Do you think we should tell the customers?" Dylan asked.

I looked at the packed dining room of people greedily shoving fried chicken into their gullets. I wanted to leave them behind. There was only so much square footage of salvation available, and I was concerned about the weight limit of the old building's rooftop. But my better judgment kicked in, and I cleared my throat, "Excuse me, patrons, I have an important announcement!"

Dylan started laughing, and I realized I had been bested yet again.

This sort of thing would continue to happen daily when working with Dylan. I was beginning to think that the guy must hate me, considering the unending humiliations he subjected me to, when out of nowhere, he gave me the best writing advice I have ever received.

In my later years at this fast food haven, I learned a lot more about responsibility. That was mainly because after I turned sixteen and moved out of the safety of my parent's rent-free home, I was forced to become self-sufficient. Except I wasn't entirely alone; after a bit of house-hopping and couch-surfing, I ended up in a small apartment with my boyfriend. He and I were what relationship gurus nowadays call toxic. We screamed at one another daily. We put each other down—he was much better at put-downs than I was, which irks me to this day. We were a lethal force to one another, and it was unclear why we stayed together for so long.

On one such day, I was contemplating this dilemma at work. I decided to write my bad boyfriend a letter explaining my misgivings about our relationship. I toiled over the letter—this was probably about the time I realized how much I love writing my significant other's letters because it allowed me to think about what I wanted to say. Much better than my usual fallback of letting word vomit spew forcefully from my mouth hole and trying to wipe that shit up before anyone walked in on the atrocity.

I asked Dylan to read what I had written to make sure it made sense. He told me it was awful. He might have been right. There were too many big words—ninety percent of which I misused. It was stark and unfeeling. It was bland.

"You gotta learn to write like you speak, Linds. This shit is unreadable. There's no way that idiot of a boyfriend will be able to get through this in one sitting. Don't think about it too hard. The best writers keep it simple."

Dylan's words stuck with me. Although he was the guy who teased me relentlessly in those early workdays, he is also the person I credit for inadvertently turning me to this dangerous and miraculous life of writing.

A few days after my conversation with Dylan, I started writing. I began the very specific act of ignoring the reality of my shitty situation and became lost in the stories I crafted from the deep and dusty crevices of my brain. I never gave the letter to my bad boyfriend. It turned out that learning how to write was far more important than working through my issues with him. On the day I packed my belongings into Janelle's car and once again ran away from a situation

I didn't know how to handle, I didn't think about how sad it was to leave the guy. Instead, I started crafting simple sentences together in my head, filing them away to scribble down at a later date.

Ten

One of the many places the bad boyfriend and I lived, was in a small one-bedroom house that had a dirt cellar. I loved that house but hated the dirt cellar. Much to the same effect, I loved our new house cat, Romeo, but strongly disliked the guy who bought me the cat. I had no money but was too comfortable at my job to go find anything new. I danced to the Time Warp in the tiny living room when nobody was home. I laughed at my own jokes and read books and decorated the kitchen with a lot of houseplants that wouldn't survive through the coming winter. And when the bad boyfriend was home, I didn't say or do much of anything at all. Living in the small house with the dirt cellar was a mixed bag of emotions, mirroring the way I felt about myself at that time.

Often, I'd find myself hand-washing our clothes in the tub and trying to come up with excuses for our landlord as to why the rent was going to be late again that month. Our frequently late rent payments were probably why our landlord didn't think it pressing to fix the toilet when it broke down. I assumed this was the penance we were meant to suffer for not paying our rent on time. We must now go without a toilet in our home. This is what happens when you are a chronic people pleaser and unable to fulfill your people pleasing tendencies. My brain kept screaming at me that I was a loser, a failure. The kind of person who couldn't even scrounge together rent money. My dumb brain convinced me, I didn't deserve a pot to piss in.

Going without a toilet wasn't the worst thing that ever happened to me. I worked early mornings at the restaurant so I could do my number two business there before any of my coworkers arrived. I have no idea where the bad boyfriend shit. Probably in the bushes in our backyard.

My days off were Mondays. Up until my day off, I just assumed I'd go without pooping that day. Couldn't be that difficult. Except it was difficult. Living below the poverty line meant I was surviving on a strict diet of leftover fried chicken foodstuffs that would otherwise be thrown out at the end of my shift. Oh, how I loved stale chicken-flavoured meat sticks and day-old wings. My bowels, unfortunately, did not love them.

Waddling anywhere is embarrassing. Waddling to work on your day off because you are about to shit your pants and that's the closest toilet your tired body can waddle to is, at best, humiliating, and at worst, well, you're about to shit your pants on a busy city sidewalk, so there's that.

"What are you doing here?" Sheri asked as I bolted in through the back door.

"Can't talk!" I yelled and ran into the staff bathroom. There I shit as I had never shit before. A deluge of heavily spiced chicken products tore through my innards and came barreling out the other end. The sounds emanating from my body were horrific, and the smells even worse. I didn't want to leave the bathroom in fear that my coworkers—or, worse, customers awaiting their order—might have overheard the travesty happening in the bathroom and wondered if someone was murdering a small rodent in there.

Alas, my own fetid stench flushed me out of the tiny room, and as I left, I went to see if Sheri needed any help on the line as I was already there and may as well help out because I'm a dedicated employee.

As I scooped some French fries into a box, I saw my coworker Lloyd approach the bathroom. Lloyd was the kind of guy you wouldn't want to run into while alone in a dark alley. Not that he was menacing, but more because he was just so weird and mysterious. Lloyd wouldn't look *at* you while he was talking, he'd look *through* you: past your eyeballs and even your soul, locating your most dire secrets and shame, exposing them for all to admire. Then he'd walk away as if nothing had ever transpired between the two of you. Lloyd. Oof, what a guy.

I wanted to shout, "No! Don't go in there," but I was too ashamed to admit the horror show inside those doors was my unholy creation. Lloyd already knew too many of my secret feelings of shame. So, I allowed poor Lloyd to unwittingly walk in on his own demise. It didn't take him long to detect the problem, and the look of pure horror and disgust on his face as he ran out of that bathroom still haunts me to this day.

Eleven

Carlee is leaving our laundry room. Carlee is leaving me. Hello childhood abandonment trauma, how nice of you to pop by. What are the chances I will ever find another coworker I feel so comfortable with? It's times like these when I wish my social anxiety was like other people's social anxiety and provided me with a monk-like muteness so I wouldn't have to converse with new people at all.

I, on the other hand, am more of a rambling fool when I get shy. This is obviously my mother's fault because Colleen Sawyer is one of the greatest conversationalists I've ever met, and subconsciously, despite my aversion to humans in general, I believe somewhere deep in my soul that I, too, must be a good conversationalist. So even though I can feel the word-and-real vomit hurdling through my body and up my throat, I provide myself with positive affirmations like, "You can do this, Lindsay!" "Ask them about their last doctor's appointment; that'll get them talking."

It's not often that I find people, much less a work environment, where I feel completely at ease. Usually, I'm a fumbling, bumbling mess of awkward pauses and long drawn-out silences after I've made everyone extremely uncomfortable going into too much detail about having to clean my dog's vulva because she refuses to clean it herself. It was a miracle I found Carlee and somehow convinced her to work with me exclusively.

Now she's going, and here begins the long hard road of learning how to converse with someone while cleaning unspeakable bodily fluids off fabrics in a laundry room made for two.

Carlee tells me her mom, Susie, is just like her, but I'm doubtful. If that were the case, that would mean there were two humans in my very own city that I don't feel an ounce of anxiety around. Seems suspect.

The thing is, I am going to have to learn how to work with someone else any way I look at it. I really want Carlee to have a change of heart and be all like, "You know what, nah. After all of these insanely hard years of working, raising two kids and putting myself through nursing school, I think I'm over it. I don't want to be a nurse anymore. I'm gonna stick to the laundry room and work with Lindsay forever."

Alas, Alberta needs as many good nurses as we can get, so, for once in my life, I'm deciding to take one for the team.

I walk into the laundry room on my first shift with Susie. She has already been rigorously trained by her daughter, and now Carlee has vanished into the oblivion of the Alberta Health Care system.

"Hi, you must be Brenna," Susie says.

Why is it I never look like myself? Seven out of ten times I meet someone new, they think I am a different person. Is it because they've read my stories and expect a glamorous writer lady instead of a short and stumpy person with a lazy eye and bad hair? Is it because my voice is deep and sultry over the phone, yet in person, I am the least sultry human one might ever encounter? I don't know why this happens; it shall remain one of the great mysteries of my life.

I consider accepting the name Brenna as my own and just being Brenna for the rest of my life while working at Lethbridge Event Rentals. I could get used to it. Eventually, though, David would call me Lindsay, and everything would go downhill from there. Susie would find out I was lying about my name and then wonder why I lied about my name, probably not understanding that the only reason I lied about my name was because I didn't want her to feel uncomfortable for getting my name wrong in the first place. The whole thing would be a total mess, so rather than changing my entire life to save us from a moment of awkwardness, I say, "I'm actually Lindsay." All the while, I'm acutely aware of how awkward it is to correct someone over something so tedious as a name.

Susie not only acts just like Carlee, but they look alike too. Same petite frame and wild eyes. Same enormous smile. I guess this happens with mothers and daughters often enough, but it always startles me to see it in real life because my mom and I look nothing alike. My mom looks fifteen years younger than her actual age, whereas I look fifteen years older. Yikes. When I'm sixty, I'm going to look seventy-five and that's going to be a real bummer man.

"So, how's Carlee doing?" I ask, and that's what gets the ball rolling. It doesn't take long to let our true colours shine because when you're stuck pressing a sea of white tablecloths, true colours are unmistakable. I learn that Susie is an ardent feminist like myself. She has no qualms about her political stances and speaks freely about the injustices she sees in the world. Susie laughs long and heartily at silly puns and loves to make raunchy jokes. I quickly understand that Carlee was right about everything. Susie is my people.

On our third shift together, Susie and I are standing back-to-back. She is bagging the hundreds of black tablecloths we have just finished ironing while I seal the bags with a Chompy Sealing Thingamajig. That's when I start to smell something horrendous.

It's a combination of rotten eggs, bad fish and body odour. It is severely unpleasant. I half turn around and wonder, *is that Susie?* As the realization hits me that I've committed to working with a smelly person for who knows how long, I see her somewhat turn around and side-eye me too. I understand by the look in her equally horrified eyes that she is thinking the exact same thing.

Then I remember the drains. Oh, thank God, the drains! I explain to my new coworker the laundry sewage situation, and Susie, as the true hero she is, takes it upon herself to become the new drain cleaner. Once again, I find myself thankful for the good and noble humans in my life.

TWELVE

Clownicer

[kloun-i-cur]

NOUN

1. An entertainer who identifies as half clown and half character.

The clownicer looked quizzically at the small child asking for a Jesus fish balloon animal because balloon art was not her specialty.

The fall of 2005 was the season I decided to sew my life back together. Running away from an abusive relationship was the first step. After finally leaving the bad boyfriend, I found lodging with Shelby, a goth chick who owned a mobile home in one of the shadier trailer parks in town.

Shelby was alright. She had a six-year-old who, I guess, was my other roommate. I didn't converse much with the kid at first. He gave me an "I see dead people" vibe, so I steered clear. I lived with Shelby and the kid from The Sixth Sense for almost a year but knew it was time to move on when I became a built-in babysitter to a child who once told me he didn't like the look of my aura.

I then moved in with a couple of gals I knew from high school. It was a much newer house than I was used to, and bigger too. Being the opportunist I am, I knew I had to snag it as soon as the offer came up. I was still working at chicken central, but knew that couldn't last forever. Intrusive thoughts about my future and career prospects kept wiggling their way into my brain.

While filtering the deep fryers one morning at the poultry plant and silently lamenting my various life failures thus far, I heard my coworker Jeff barge in through the back door. Jeff was a metalhead with hair twice as long as mine and the gentlest demeanour imaginable.

"Hey Linds, I found this flyer on my way to work today." He handed me a ratty piece of paper.

"SYLVAN LAKE YOUTH INITIATIVE PROGRAM," it read.

"What is it?" I asked.

"I dunno, it's like something for dropouts and shit," he replied. Oh, sweet, sweet Jeff.

Upon further examination, I learned if you were a young person between sixteen and twenty-one and lived in central Alberta, you were allowed to enroll. The application process would be held at the Seventh-Day Adventist church the following Monday.

We called it the Program. It was an alternative learning plan for wilful teens no longer in school. It provided a place to go every weekday and roadmap one's life. Most of us were high school dropouts, drug addicts or wayward souls looking for a path. You know, run-of-the-mill teenage dirtbags—as the song might have you believe. Yet something buried deep within told us we might do better. We learned basic skills like building a resume and what this GED thing was all about.

The best part about the program was that we were paid to go there. It was like three bucks an hour or something, but they paid us, so I signed up immediately. The friends I made in the Program were so important at that time in my life. Almost all of us came from difficult situations. We huddled in a sparsely furnished church attic where our daily classes were held, and we held each other up. From single moms to abused teens to drug addicts and those of us who had lost our way, we revelled in one another's triumphs and encouraged each other through the challenges. It was the other kids who taught me the most in that program. The facilitators were apt to bring religion into their lesson plans, and being realists, they continually tried pushing me into attainable job postings like childcare. I kept asking them why I would leave my sweet fast food job to look after snot-nosed kids. They thought a career in childcare was more respectable, I guess.

What I wanted to do was become a writer. They shot that idea down immediately. Writers don't drop out of high school. Writers don't run away from home at sixteen. Writers don't pin up weird wall dolls as apartment décor and name them Fred and talk to them while they're high on mushrooms about the magnificence of Bob Saget. But that's another story. Maybe writers should do all those things. It sure makes for some great material.

One girl in the program wasn't a dropout or a druggie or teen-mom. Sarah had graduated the year before and was the most intelligent and put-together of the group. Sarah was going places. I don't know why she was even there. The rest of us were runaways or came from terrible homes. We smoked joints in the parking lot in the morning before class and constantly razzed the teachers to let us out for another cigarette break. Not Sarah though; Sarah was my polar opposite. Beautiful and intelligent, she probably went on to be an environmental lawyer. Sarah was always nearby, just lurking and listening. She befriended me right off the bat, and that year, while we attended the Program together and hung out daily, I continued to quietly wonder why someone as gifted as her would choose to hang out with a dirtbag like me.

Six months into the Program, I was living with my two friends from high school and still feeling incredibly lucky to have scored such sweet living accommodations. My bedroom was in the basement that doubled as the expansive laundry room, which must have been annoying to my roommates, who had to deal with my sty-like living quarters each time they wanted to do a load of laundry. There was a spare room available upstairs, but because I've always been an antisocial homebody, I figured it best to hole up in the basement where I'd be less likely to have to deal with company invited over by my more extroverted roomies.

One February morning, eyes bleary and filled with the sandy stuff I like to call squidgets, I awoke to Sarah leaning over my bed, softly saying, "Lindsay, wake up. You're late for class!"

"Gah!" I screamed. "What in the love of fuck are you doing here?"

After a late night of watching *The Rocky Horror Picture Show* on repeat and eating every variety of five-cent candy known to man, I had developed a pretty rough sugar hangover and slept through my alarm, still bleeping faintly in the background. In my brain-shrivelled state, I must have tossed my parka over the clock, muffling the sound just enough for me to fall back into a dreamless slumber.

"I knew you had probably just slept in, so I came to get you. Being a little tired isn't worth losing your spot in the program. Now get up, and let's get going."

One of the program facilitators, Michelle, had founded a nonprofit that helped fund extracurricular activities for low-income children. It was a straight-up clown college. I signed up immediately. We went through rigorous clown training. Believe me when I tell you, there are many rules to learn when becoming a mythical creature such as a clown.

Rules While Clowning

    1. NO DRINKING

    2. NO EATING

    3. NO SWEARING

    4. NO TALKING POLITICS

    5. SUPPRESS YOUR ENCROACHING DEPRESSIVE STATE

    6. NO USE OF SEXUALLY EXPLICIT INNUENDOES

    7. NO CRIMINAL BEHAVIOUR

I'M NOT THE MANAGER HERE

8. MAINTAIN CHARACTER ATTRIBUTES

9. NO PICKING FIGHTS

10. NO PICKING WEDGIES

Once you had built your clown, or clownicer in my case, and were at an event, you must stay in character. By breaking the magic in any way, you risked allowing the normies to find out you weren't that character but just some weirdo dressed up as a clown.

Here enters Lola Cunningham the Third. I chose to create a "clownicer" because the idea of a fictional character crossed with a clown persona fed my need for uniqueness, and also, I didn't have the money to purchase a clown nose at that time. I taught many children how to craft a simplistic balloon animal while moonlighting as Lola. During uneventful weekdays, our clowning troupe would give slapdash lessons to kids who wanted to learn the art of clowning.

The most exciting experiences while clowning came from when we were asked to entertain patrons at local rodeos and farmer's markets. We were hired to rile up the people walking the grounds and get them excited about the day's events, but mostly, we just scared passersby. We'd set up a table during farmer's markets to lure small children into our clowning culture.

On one occasion at an indoor farmer's market, I had been burning the midday oil. Oh, how tired I was, having worked for three hours straight without a break. Don't clownicers have worker's rights too? I decided I would sneak out behind the building for a smoke. Sarah gave me a grave look and said, "I hope you're not about to break character, Lola," in her shitty southern accent, which wasn't nearly as well-researched as my equally terrible British accent.

"Oh, bollocks," I said, not understanding what that meant but figuring it sounded right. I slunk around the building and lit that sweet ciggy as soon as I was out of sight.

Then I heard, "Oh man, dude, you seeing this?" I looked up and saw two, er, how should I say this—two men of bedraggled nature. Yes, let's call it bedraggledness. They must have been in their mid-forties, and their clothes looked as though they might have stood erect and body-like even without a body within them. One was holding a teeny tiny baggie in his hand containing a substance of questionable nature. I stared at the men long and hard, wondering what to do in this strange situation. They, in turn, stared at me and intermittently looked at one another. Even though I was smoking, my clown training reminded me not to break character more than I already had.

I didn't know then that this would be one of my final clowning adventures. I didn't quit clowning because I grew weary of the job, but instead, as I was meant to, I learned how to make my way in this big 'ol world.

It's funny how a sheet of paper handed to me by a coworker about a youth initiative program changed my entire life path. That program led to clowning and clowning gave me the courage to start over. I began earning more money and found an apartment I could afford on my own. I started to heal from the wounds endured through the bad years. I learned how to stand on my own two feet. My new life started in oversized big red shoes, which gave me the balance to begin walking into the future.

The two men and I kept up our silent staring contest until I was done with my smoke, and as I turned to leave, I said in my terrible British accent, "Cheerio boys, hope you have a lovely trip!"

Thirteen

I just stuck my hand in a slick of Cheez Whiz and was reminded of that time an ex-boyfriend wanted to bring this particular product into the bedroom as a part of some weird kink. That was about the time he became an ex. No judgment, man. Food kinks are cool and all, but Cheez Whiz?

Part of my job description as a laundry wench is to count the returned linen items and get them ready for cleaning. This entails lugging enormous hard plastic boxes from the back loading dock to the laundry area of the warehouse. From there, we confirm the correct number of napkins, tablecloths, and drapes have been returned from their various events; then, we colour-code them into their correct dirty laundry bins, where they await washing.

If there's one thing I can rely on in this quickly devolving world, it's that my laundry orders will be returned as if a band of drunken raccoons had been having one hell of an orgy within them. The boxes come back filled with some of the most heinous fine linens I have ever seen.

If you ever witness someone at a wedding spitting their half-chewed prime rib into a linen napkin and then balling it up never to be thought of again, please slap that mother fucker with your duelling glove. The half-chewed food I've had to scrape out of napkins before washing them could fill a child's toy box, and that's a lot of mouth food I'd be putting into some random child's toy box.

And God save us from the glow sticks. Glow sticks may seem like an excellent idea for wedding favours to help get the party started, but please don't allow the inquisitive eight-year-old at your table to slice open said glow stick and finger paint all over a white polyester tablecloth. That shit doesn't come out, and the glowing goo can't be healthy for the kid. I once found the phrase, "Hello Everyone," written with thick black Sharpie marker in the perfect bubbled text of a teenager on an ivory-coloured tablecloth. If your fourteen-year-old writes on linen tablecloths, you've raised her wrong.

I've seen the aftermath of guests who have allowed their small muddy-pawed dogs to romp over vintage lace overlays, and I don't know what was in that mud, but it took hours of scrubbing to get out. I've come across boxes and boxes of covert confetti that peppers our warehouse floor when pulling out drapes from their return boxes. I'm still finding golden-coloured "Hitched" confetti in the corners of the dish pit from the summer of 2021.

I'm not sure how the cheese came to be on the tablecloth because I'm confident it was Cheez Whiz, and who is eating processed cheese spread at a wedding? Either way, an unsuspecting handful of bright orange goop is not how I want to begin my shift. Something about unsuspectingly touching food served over seventy-two hours before makes a person die a little inside.

"Ugh!" I scream, "I just stuck my hand in some sort of spreadable cheese."

Susie is busy bagging napkins into twenty-five counts and can't hear me over the press and washer running.

"Pardon me?" she yells.

"There's fermenting cheese stuck to these tablecloths," I bellow.

"Ew," is all she answers. Susie has a much greater tolerance for the gross part of our job. A while back, we had some bed sheets come in from a B&B we contract for, and Susie told me there was an enormous shit stain on one.

"Well, at least I think that's what it was," she told me as I listened with rapt attention. "It looked like the guests had tried to wash it out in the bathtub, but I'm pretty sure it was shit."

"Oh my God," was all I could reply, such was the nature of my awe.

"My guess is there was some anal going on, and someone let loose." She said it with such assurance that I genuinely believed no other explanation was possible. And it made sense; there you are on your wedding night in an adorable little bed and breakfast, gooned out of your mind, and you think, 'Hey, why not? There's a first time for everything!' Little did you know, you would literally shit the bed. And here I am, cleaning up other people's poor decisions. At least they rinsed the sheets.

When I worked at the fast food joint, cleaning the grease trap was one of our greatest punishments. I suspect grease trap cleaning is automated these days (damn robots taking our jobs!), but we had to go at it by hand back in the day.

The grease from the fryers would collect in this wretched little floor burrow beneath the dish pit. The unlucky soul tasked with cleaning the trap would have to use a large scooper and spoon out the top layer of grease, discarding the bad-smelling stuff into a garbage bag, then dump that into the grease bin at the back of the store.

I can't remember why I was in trouble. Perhaps that was the time Jamie and I were caught getting handsy with each other in the chicken cooler. The point is I had been ordered to clean the grease trap. I wrangled my friend Tasha into helping me, and together, we set upon our task.

The worst part of the grease trap was the smell. That floating repugnant top layer of grease stank like a cow had burped into a fermenting bag of feces and doused the entire thing in the juice from a tuna can. While enduring this cleaning regiment, we ran multiple fans and propped open the back door of the building despite it being a cold Canadian January morning. The restaurant getting a whiff of the grease trap would surely clear out our customers in a hurry.

Tash and I had fashioned a grease receptacle out of a cardboard box lined with a garbage bag to ensure nothing leaked through the sides. As we finished up, our nose holes plugged with wads of paper towel, we each picked up one side of the box and made our way out to the grease bin. As we were walking, and the putrid grease was that much closer to my face, I realized how stupid the blocking of our nostrils really was. Because now, my only way to breathe was through my mouth, which meant I had to taste the rotting sludge of chicken death rather than smell it. Fantastic.

"Okay, on the count of three, we'll lift and dump into the bin."

"One, two, three..."

We lifted; alas, we never had the chance to dump. As soon as the box was chest level, the bottom gave way, causing the bag of rancid fat and lard to plummet to the ground and explode in one extremely unfortunate bomb of grease. We were drenched from the waist down. The smell seeped into my skin and stayed there for weeks, no matter how hard I tried to scrub it off. I learned a valuable lesson that I've never forgotten to this day: always hold the bottom of the box.

I now think about the grease trap as I scrub soft cheese from beneath my fingernails. Having to deal with the occasional food remnant or anal leakage stain is a bummer (yep, I went there), but at least I'm no longer taking grease trap showers.

Fourteen

"Your thigh is twice the size of a ham hock, Leslie. What have your parents been feeding you, girl?" the chef asked as she smeared on the cooling gel and wrapped a bandage around my scalded inner thigh. I reminded her my name was Lindsay, not Leslie, and she replied by ignoring me. Moments before, I was running hot water out of the industrial sink faucet. I leaned over to turn off the tap when the spout hooked into my apron and steaming hot water ran down the fabric and directly onto my stomach and thigh. Hello, second-degree burns.

I don't know why this woman was so obsessed with my weight. My weight wasn't impeding my job in the slightest. I could run a flight of stairs and regularly performed impromptu dance parties (by myself) in the pantry. I could mash a pot of spuds with relative ease. I could haul the five gallon pail of pickles from the cooler to the line even though I despised doing so. I was pretty happy with my body. That was, until my chef made it clear that my body shape disgusted her as she applied first aid to my boiled skin.

You might wonder why I was standing half-naked in front of a chef instead of being rushed to the emergency room. I had decided to take a break from the chicken world and try my hand at making some real money. Real money in Alberta meant working the rigs. Of course, my weak constitution and lack of upper body strength did not bode well for me getting a job as a roughneck, so instead I was cooking in a remote northern Alberta oilfield camp. It was a two-hour drive to the nearest tiny town, and I doubt they had an ER there. Instead, we had a medic on site who was pretty useless, so we dealt with burns and minor injuries ourselves—with the added benefit of inflicting verbal abuse on the victim.

My first impression of Chef was not a good one. Between the burn on my skin and Chef's dank burns on my soul I was quickly regretting my choice to come work in this northern hell hole. In the days to come, she would call me every name she could think of that began with the letter L. None of them being Lindsay.

I got the job the same way most well-paid positions are attained—nepotism. At the time, my dad was a well-known drilling consultant in the field and made a few phone calls on my behalf.

I wasn't excited about working on a secluded drilling site with nobody I knew and a horrible woman I was forced to call Chef. But I was determined to make a go of it. I had never exhibited a love for cooking, and still didn't, but when you are young and have an oil-rich province in front of you, money talks. What mattered most to me was that my dad was finally proud of something I was doing.

Up until this point, I had only been a disappointment, what with running away from home and shacking up with the bad boyfriend and all. Dad and I were not on the best of terms.

Then, out of nowhere, he mentioned getting me a prep-cook position in a rig camp, and without taking any time to consider, I said, "Yeah, that sounds like a fantastic idea!"

I look remarkably similar to my dad. This has always been a sore spot for me because what young woman wants to hear that she looks identical to her middle-aged father?

Many of Dad's drilling associates would take one look at me while I was restocking the mashed potatoes on the line and say, "Hey, you've got a Sawyer look about you. Any chance you're related to Dan?"

"Yep, he's my dad," I'd reply unenthusiastically. They did not understand the distinct sort of indignity that comes with a complete stranger looking at your face and saying, "Hello, eighteen-year-old girl, you remind me of a balding, pot bellied guy I once knew; tell me, are you him?"

On the bright side, this meant the guys immediately took a shine to me and, from then on, were always chatting me up. When I refer to them as "the guys," that's what they were. I'm not being sexist, since the only women in the camp were Chef, the useless medic, and me. This was back in the early 2000s, and mega companies weren't yet "diversifying" by hiring three women and a black guy to meet their yearly quota.

The light conversation with the rig workers all seemed perfectly natural. From the time I was small, my dad was inviting his rigging pals to hang out with our family on days off. Gruff and tumble riggers were a part of my everyday adolescent life.

Unfortunately, to Chef, my talking to the men meant that I was sleeping with all of them: the young ones, the ancient old dudes who could have been my grandfather, and that one guy I'm pretty sure was gay. Even the grocery truck driver when I told him we were missing a case of cantaloupes. As we all know, mentioning cantaloupes in casual conversation is a stellar pickup line. According to Chef, every man that crossed my path was a bone to jump.

On my second week there, Chef pulled me aside to insinuate that I was "having relations" with every penis in camp. She told me that this sort of behaviour just wasn't done. This was a serious job; if I couldn't act professionally, I'd be on the next grocery truck out of there. My reaction, of course, was to laugh. The thought was absurd. Every chance Chef got, she told me that I was too fat or slutty or terrible at the job. No, I wasn't the best prep cook. I didn't discover my love for cooking until late into my twenties, and I was a mere eighteen years old in this timeline. Still, I came prepared every day with new salad recipes to try and peeled a bucket of potatoes in record time.

Despite the bullying, I wasn't going to stop conversing with the new friends I'd made. The idea of not talking to people was inconceivable to me. It didn't take long for Chef to have enough of my "insubordination". Insubordination, as in saying hi to Jeremy at the dinner table or watching the Simpsons with Bill in the rec hall during my afternoon break. After a few days of me laughing at her slut-shaming, she ran me off the rig. For the layman, getting run-off means that your department head speaks to the higher-ups with concerns about your work habits, and because I was nothing but a cog in the machine, they decided to ship me out on the next grocery truck.

Usually, staff would be bussed together with each shift change. I would have to hitch a premature ride with the supply truck that afternoon.

I was outraged. How could that old bag of bones do this to me? I needed that job, and the money was better than anything I had ever earned. I tried complaining to some of the guys I had befriended from the camp, but they turned their backs to me, showing solidarity with the one who cooked their steaks. It was a brutal reality to face, but the truth is, no amount of pleasant small talk can beat a perfectly grilled porterhouse.

The grocery truck driver felt for me though, and listened to my woes as we sped down the highway and back to civilization. I didn't have a cell phone back then, so when we stopped at a saloon in Clyde, I found a payphone to call my parents to let them know what happened.

"Please pick up, Mom, please pick up," I whispered to myself and the telephone gods as I waited for either my mom or dad to answer. I felt things wouldn't go great if I had to reveal the occurrences of the last 24 hours to my dad.

"Yello," Dad said.

I hesitantly told my father I'd been run off the site and was now sitting in a dodgy bar with a strange man I didn't know. We had both been drinking quite heavily at this point, so I was stuck in this place for the foreseeable future. Also, I had no money.

It was about a two-hour drive from the Clyde saloon back home to my parent's house, and as I got in Dad's truck and mentally prepared for a stern talking to about responsibility, Dad surprised me by laughing.

"I've known my fair share of Chefs, and some of those old bitties up in camp can be real battle axes."

Dad and I never had much to say to one another on any given occasion, but we agreed that following in Dad's footsteps with oilfield work didn't seem like my best bet. He seemed fine, happy even, with this quiet revelation. Once upon a time, Dad was forced into an oilfield lifestyle and I don't think he wanted the same for me. We drove down the moonlit QE 2 highway, casually chatting about our camp days (his being much more extensive than mine) and what I might try next for employment opportunities.

Fifteen

As I concentrate on not creasing the floor-length navy tablecloth we are folding, Susie is passionately rhapsodizing about women's rights. She does this all the time. I tell her my woes, and she sympathizes, explaining that a large chunk of these issues would be solved if people would just start taking feminism more seriously. She's the kind of women's libber that we all should be. Loud, strident and extremely informed. She's also beautiful, inside and out, which probably helps her cause—it usually does with these things. People always want to listen to attractive humans. At least I do.

Look, I'm totally for women's rights. Feminism all the way, dude! Most days, I can't wait to smash the patriarchy with our awesome ideas from these big ol' brain-bags. Today though, I'm thinking about other things.

Susie doesn't notice that I'm only half listening to her passionate ranting. She doesn't judge me for letting my mind wander. That's another thing the laundry room does to a person; it allows for abstract thinking. There's something about the steam that billows out of the press after feeding it damp king-sized sheets that massage ideas to the surface. The humid air and stacks of tall linen napkins awaiting bagging create the perfect environment for brainstorming. Even the nastiness atop the unlaundered hotel bedding gives me hope for creative lawlessness.

I'm thinking about the career proposal David has just given me. He wants me to take more responsibility for the laundry room. I will be the head of the laundry room. The woman in charge. I will order the washing machine's chemicals and ensure the press and sealer get their annual maintenance checks. I will figure out what that weird smell from the drains is. The bay where our warehouse is located used to be a meat processing plant, so perhaps there's some rotting sausage down there. That's my number one hypothesis at the moment.

Responsibility doesn't come easy to me. I don't like it, and I don't want it. Being accountable does not top the list of things I see for myself in this business. Once upon a time, I was responsible for an entire sandwich company. Did not end well.

"What's bothering you?" Susie finally asks when she realizes that I haven't consumed a single word she's been saying. I've been doing that thing where you nod along, even though what the person is saying does not warrant a nodding kind of response.

"You know how we recently swapped plastic suppliers?" I ask Susie.

"Yeah."

"Well when I called the old supplier and told them we had decided to go another way, the guy totally lost it. He got all huffy on the phone badmouthing the new company and it was so cringy and awkward," I explain. "If I take this laundry room supervisor position, or whatever we want to call it, I'm going to have to deal with this kind of shit all the time."

"Yeah I guess you're right," Susie says, "but I'm here to help you now, and together, we can do anything."

My favourite thing about Susie is one minute she can be joking about splooge on the bedding and in the next breath she sounds like an after-school special saying we should reach for the stars.

Part 2: Red Deer

Sixteen

Dear faceless man to whom I spoke over the phone eighteen years ago,

Thank you for your candidness. I rarely experience such creative threats over the phone, and for that, I will forever hold you in my memory. The day had begun rather eventless. I woke up, took my morning shot of vodka to get through the day, and bussed to my job downtown as a customer service representative for a wireless company.

For the next eight hours, I answered calls from customers waiting in queues varying between twenty minutes to three hours. Oh, how I loved speaking to clients who had been listening to shitty radio music for the past two hours. The combination of terrible top 40s and long wait times gave them ample opportunity to grow irate about the long-distance charges on their bill.

You were enraged that you had ordered a subscription via your phone's limited internet service—*Cool Ringtones Monthly*, as I recall—and were under the impression at the time of purchase that it was a one-time charge. However, you angrily advised me that it had been charged to your bill for two months. The injustice of it all!

I explained that this was a third-party charge, and although the payment does come off your bill, it wasn't the mobile company charging you.

You disagreed.

I broke down the explanation and tried again.

You argued that a "dumb twat falafel" like myself couldn't understand the logistics of the billing department; thus, you needed to speak with my manager.

As with many multimillion-dollar corporations, the management trained us lowly phone operators to summon them only if the situation became dire. Our motto as the floor peons was to deescalate, deescalate, deescalate.

So, deescalate, I tried.

"I apologize for the inconvenience, sir; unfortunately, I have no control over this charge. We value you as a customer, so I am happy to discount your next month's bill with the incurred charges. You will have to contact the Cool Ringtone Monthly people to cancel your subscription."

It was your response to my pitch that genuinely changed the course of my life as I know it, and for that reason alone, I felt the need all these years later to write this letter and thank you from the bottom of what you might refer to as my idiotic soul-sack.

"You stupid little bitch. Do you know who I am?"

Me, interrupting you: "Why yes, sir, you are Mr. Meatbag Huffington and...."

"And I've been with this mobile company for five years! Five years, do you hear that? Five years of hardly ever missing a payment, and you don't value my business enough to get this issue fixed for me? What kind of a piss poor shithole are you running over there?"

My detection of mockery was no match for your advanced wit, so I foolishly answered, "Oh, I'm sorry, Mr. Huffington, I have nothing to do with running this business."

This comment was the breaking point for you.

"You must be the dimmest woman to have ever walked God's green Earth. I want to feel your head under my boot. Jesus, the fuckin' things I'd do to you, you'd be screaming for mercy." You began breathing heavily into the phone, and it occurred to me that you were trouble.

I hung up on you immediately and spoke directly to my superiors. I wanted to ensure that our employee records and the location of our call center weren't public access—for obvious reasons. Not obvious enough, it seemed, because rather than getting any comfort from the higher-ups, I received a stern talking to because I had hung up on a customer. I was told that I should have transferred the call to a supervisor when things had initially gotten heated—dismissing previous teachings that we should do everything in our power not to transfer up.

As an outsider looking in, I can see why many people would think it silly of me to write you a thank you letter right now. The thing is, I believe in my heart of hearts that you deserve this.

You deserve to know that after that experience, I quit the call center job. I taught myself to say no to a string of ever-devolving lousy relationships. My backbone and thighs grew thicker, and I learned to love and flaunt them in equal measure. Your blatant verbal abuse of a total stranger was like magic to me. It allowed me to throw away the rose-tinted glasses and acknowledge all the bat shit crazy misogynistic bullshit that happens all around me every day.

It taught me how to laugh at the despicable commentary I sometimes receive on my articles. And how not to dwell on the fact that male writers, writing about the same things, do not receive nearly as many diminishing replies in their comment sections. I never thought about you much in the years to come, but I did think about the women in your life, and they inspired me to speak up when vulnerable people were being mistreated.

Sure, you can't take credit for all my unapologetic feminism. I've got plenty of bad boyfriends and daddy issues that have contributed their fair share, but our conversation got the ball rolling.

I now ensure that my workplaces practice reliable protocols regarding their employees' physical and emotional well-being. I am no longer too shy to argue with upper management about bad business practices. I no longer drown my worries and fear about "my image" in the bottom of a vodka bottle because I've learned over the years that a good old fashion No Fucks Given approach to the patriarchy does just fine while also saving one's liver.

I laugh long and heartily, knowing that you are the sort of person who believes that some humans are genuinely superior to others, and yet it was your actions that day that planted this seed of power within me. You reinforced lingering, messy ideas that floated haphazardly around my brain that I am strong and never need anyone else's acceptance for validation. The irony of this event and its repercussions is so sweet that I giggle with giddiness while writing you this letter. A strange man who tried to bully a young girl into getting his way instead forced her to grow into the kind of woman who would fight endlessly for his victims.

This letter is not to praise your actions that day, Mr. Meatbag Huffington; it is to thank you and remind you that every word, thought, and intention you put into this world will always return to you. Whether you approve of it or not.

I hope that every woman disparaged, broken, and scared by a man like you will also know the absolute satisfaction of taking that pain and growing larger than life from it.

Seventeen

Finally, I was in my very own apartment. I moved into a bachelor suite in Red Deer, a neighbouring city to my hometown of Sylvan Lake and loved the freedom that living alone offered. Until then, I had only lived with roommates, but I found a cheap enough place to rent on my own. Granted, the apartment was one large room with a bathroom and a tiny kitchen with a refrigerator not much bigger than those beer fridges you sometimes see in the kinds of garages that hold everything but cars—but I was still overjoyed with my setup.

Every day I hauled my hungover ass out of bed, dressed, and lazily ambled to the bus stop to hitch a ride across the city to my customer service job at the wireless company.

Working as a faceless number for a large corporation is a beautiful and horrifying thing. On the one hand, you don't need to impress the company because the company has no clue who you are. Sure, your supervisors know you. And maybe one or two managers could conjure up your name if pressed, but the CEO of that place? They wouldn't be able to pick you out of a lineup. Thus, attempting to impress the bigwigs was a fool's errand.

Talking down angry cell phone customers is only as fun as you make it. Sure, if you take the guy who screams that he wants to curb stomp your face seriously because you don't have the authority to reverse third-party billing charges, the job might be a big ole bummer. But knowing when you could use your unique power of reimbursement to your kind customers' advantage made the entire job worth it.

Usually, customers were angry about unknown charges on their bills. Sometimes they wanted me to give them a half-price rate on the newest cell phone on the market. Most of the time, they were lonely shut-ins who just wanted to chat. These were, by far, my favourite calls. I was good at this job. Not because I have computer skills or am customer service savvy but because I'm a people pleaser. *Excuse me, nice lady who keeps calling me sweetie, you can't pay both your cell phone bill and your rent this month? Allow me to slap a seventy-dollar credit on your account for no reason whatsoever. I'll figure out the details later.*

That was the good part of the job. Getting to hear the relieved cries of strangers when I could help them out of a tight spot was like a siren song to me. I did this way too often. I'm surprised I lasted at that job as long as I did.

Except, I'm not really surprised at all because I made the brilliant move of getting romantically involved with one of my trainers at work. After I was done with the training part of the job, my instructor Blaine and I exchanged numbers and started a flirty daily text exchange, even though that shit cost me ten cents per message. Man, was I ever thirsty back then.

Blaine was several years older than me and pretty much my exact opposite with his left-brained, analytical thinking. He scoffed at my constant silliness and often asked me strange questions about the psychology of life. Things like if you were a sandwich, what sandwich would you be? What was this? A job interview? But obviously, the answer is a loaded bunwich because I like big buns and I cannot lie.

One August afternoon when I was least expecting it, Blaine texted me and asked if I wanted to go out for ice cream.

"Holy macaroni sticks!" I screamed to my long-time friend, Janelle. It wasn't surprising I was with Janelle when Blaine texted me. At that time, we were mostly always together. "He wants to take me on a date!" I didn't drive at the time, so as is the requirement of any wing-woman, Janelle zipped me down to the agreed-upon Dairy Queen where Blaine had suggested we meet.

She looked me up and down before I got out of her car and said these words to me, "Just don't be fucking weird, okay?" And as is my tendency, I disappointed her immediately.

I was looking pretty darn cute in my flowing, hippy-style skirt. I tripped over the curb as I stepped out of her car, but luckily caught myself before my skirt flipped up and flashed my underwear to the windowed dining room of the Dairy Queen.

An accidental ass-flashing had happened to me a few years before when I was with Janelle and walking into West Edmonton Mall with a parking lot full of thousands of eager mall-goers. The experience taught me that my best friend would ruthlessly laugh until she cried at any of my foibles, no matter the circumstance.

Inside, Blaine was wearing his trademark button-down blue and white plaid number with the short sleeves. He was only missing a few pens and a pair of specs jutting out from the breast pocket. I noted that he did not comment on my adorable appearance.

We ordered our cones and sat down in the air-conditioned dining room. We chatted about work and all the people we mutually hated. It's so fun to talk about similar dislikes with someone you're getting to know. Just when you thought you were the only person on the planet who inwardly shuddered when having to sit beside coke-head Cam because of his penchant for screaming at little old ladies who couldn't follow instructions, you learn that everyone loathes that big nostriled bastard.

Then I dropped my ice cream into Blaine's lap and the entire afternoon went straight to shit. Why did I choose to sit next to him rather than across from him, like any normal person would have? What did I think was going to happen? *Hey mister I hardly know; allow me to sit beside you so I can give you the ole handy johnson in this DQ window booth?* Gah.

Most guys would have been all like, Oh, that's fine, don't worry about it, I'll go clean off, because aren't we living in a perpetual rom-com meet-cute situation? Not Blaine. He lived firmly in reality. He scolded me like I was a child.

"You need to be more careful, Lindsay! You're always leaping before you look, and then accidents happen," he said. "This is exactly like last week when you hung up on that customer who insulted the register of your voice."

"He said I sounded exactly like his chain-smoking uncle! I'm sorry, but that was rude. Assholes like that don't deserve my customer service."

Blaine looked around nervously, then quietly said, "Can you please watch your language?"

"Okay, Dad."

"That's disgusting," he said coldly.

I should have called him out on his behaviour, but in those early years of adulthood, it hadn't been my way. I was apt to dilute myself to appear more palatable to men. At an early age, I found my hyperactive personality and non-filtered word vomit were a turn-off to most people in general. Have you heard? Apparently, wild women aren't everyone's taste! Nowadays, I try not to change myself for anyone, but back when I was young and drowning in insecurity, I admit I was often not myself.

As the man droned on about new cell phones on the market, I found my thoughts drifting toward the half bag of crunchy Cheetos back at the apartment. They were calling my name. *"Lindsay,"* they cheered from their home in the cupboard behind the soy sauce, *"We yearn for the chance to brighten your fingers with our sumptuous orange dust."* I laughed out loud at my little daydream, and it was at that point I realized this new love interest wasn't of interest at all.

Blaine seemed just as relieved to get rid of me when I finally asked him to drive me home. As we hopped into his car, he said, "Okay, what's your address?"

Silence.

What *was* my address? I had only lived there for a few weeks and hadn't imprinted the numbers to memory yet. "I can't remember," I said with as much grit as I could muster. I was bound and determined not to let him get me down again.

"What do you mean you can't remember?"

"I honestly don't know. I haven't memorized it yet."

"Okay, so just give me directions on how to get there then."

Silence.

"You do know how to get to your house, right?" he asked.

Technically I did not.

I hadn't paid attention to where Janelle was driving when she brought me to the Dairy Queen earlier, and I had no clue where we were in the city. I remain directionally challenged to this day, so it was not surprising this indignity had befallen me.

"Well, I can probably find it if we drive to the college," I spat, trying to be fierce.

"Lindsay, the college is across the city. This is insane! You should know where you live."

His words burnt into my soul the way a hotdog stick sears through a wiener on a hot summer's night. We drove around fruitlessly for half an hour, silently stewing in each other's presence and intermittently crying, "Is that the turn?"

Finally, I called Janelle on my Nokia and asked her to direct us back to my apartment. It turns out we were only a few blocks from my house, so I've got to say I did all right in the end. The entire experience taught me that I will go to great lengths to quell the loneliness of moving to a new city. And also, loneliness isn't so bad when the alternative is a guy who just doesn't get you.

Eighteen

There are specific "learning moments" we all experience growing up. Times when we know, without a shadow of a doubt, the exact situation we are facing will provide us with insight on how *not* to do things in the future. As I hovered over my bathroom sink, triple-lined with plastic grocery bags, and proceeded to explode with diarrhea, I realized this was one of those moments.

But let's rewind to Blaine for a moment.

The Blaine thing was a definite setback in the new and extraordinary life I was carving out for myself, but I wasn't going to let that keep me down. A few weeks after the indignity of forgetting my own address, I had regrouped and was ready to play the field again.

I was quickly learning that the greatest thing about living on your own is the newfound sense of privacy. This meant having the ability to walk around naked and no more hanging a bra on the door handle if you're getting busy with a new beau. And getting frisky was precisely my plan for the evening. An old acquaintance was coming over, and I was going to make him dinner. My idea of making dinner was a large bowl of air-popped popcorn and some beers on the side. Hashtag chef's kiss.

I'll spare you the gritty deets, but let's just say the popcorn acted as an aphrodisiac. Afterwards, he promptly got up and went to the bathroom to dispose of the condom. I headed that way after he was done and thought, *huh, that's weird, I wonder where he tossed the rubber* when glancing at the empty trash can. The notion was fleeting though, as I remembered there was talk about going downtown for some sushi (not a euphemism). If there's one thing that can distract me from any train of thought, it's the idea of shoving sashimi down my pie hole.

That night I fell into the kind of intoxicated sleep one gets when embarking on a great adventure. Of course, I reckoned the adventure would be a new relationship. The universe had something else in mind.

At about 3 a.m., I woke to a foul smell and the sound of gurgling drain pipes. I made my way to the bathroom and found my bathtub and toilet backed up and overflowing with poo. Human poo. A chunky brown liquid filled both porcelain basins to the brim. The unbearable smell hit me, followed closely by the realization that this couldn't be my shit alone but the collective crap packets of the entire second floor of the apartment building. I cried out in horror.

Then, as if working in divine intervention, the most unfortunate rumbling began in my stomach. It seemed that the sushi wasn't sitting well. I weighed my options.

Should I knock on a neighbours' door? I hardly knew them and both couples living on either side of my apartment did not like me due to my pot smoking and partying. Nowadays, this would not deter me from asking to use someone's shitter, but back then, being young, and quite frankly mortified by the hard decisions I was facing, I knew that knocking on my neighbour's door was going to have to be a hard no.

As I looked back and forth from my fecal-infested bathroom to the balcony and then to my kitchen sink, my stomach cramps grew more dire by the second. I knew I must figure out a plan fast, lest I shit my pants in a bathroom that was already full-to-bursting with human waste. That's how I ended up blowing up my sink with the explosive kind of diarrhea that only comes from too much beer combined with questionable sushi. After I was done my business, I felt marginally better—physically, at least—so I called my landlord and told him we had a problem.

He had already received calls from both my neighbours on that floor as they, too, had poop travelling up their drains in an extraordinary fashion. I disposed of my secret bag of feces by sleuthing through the dead of night to the dumpster located in the parking lot. All the while desperately hoping that no one witnessed my biohazardous waste disposal methods.

My mind whirred with the mantra, 'Noooo, this can't be happening!' as I watched suited-up plumbers fix the issue by snaking the apartment's drains. Finally, after a long, trying night of too many indignities to count, a condom was found to be the culprit. I played dumb and asked, "Who would be stupid enough to flush a condom down the drain?" But what I was quietly asking myself was, "Who would be stupid enough to sleep with a guy who doesn't know how to dispose of a condom properly?"

Sometimes we take our losses and own them fully. We scream from the rooftop, "Yes, I forgot where my own home was located," and "Yes, I had to shit into a bag in my sink because I had explosive diarrhea and no working toilet!" These admissions grow us as human beings. Alas, at that time in my life, I was not a fully formed woman. So instead of owning up to my crimes, I left that beautiful apartment. I packed my belongings into exactly one duffle bag and skipped the province, hoping to outrun the devastating memories of days past.

Part 3: Victoria

Nineteen

The duffle bag was packed tight with brightly coloured clothing. It was 2006, I was a ripe twenty-year-old and moving to Victoria, BC. Mom and Dad drove me across one and a half provinces from our hometown in Sylvan Lake. It was the first time in a long time that we were getting along.

I was shacking up with my Great Grandma Jean, my dad's grandmother and the oldest human being I had ever met. Well, I hadn't actually met her yet. According to my mom, I had met her. Briefly, at my paternal grandmother's funeral several years before, but my drug-addled brain at the time refused to keep the encounter firmly implanted in my memory. So, by my approximation, I had never met the woman.

Upon arriving at the apartment building in the Esquimalt district of the city, my dad threatened my life, saying, "You better not make us regret this, Lindsay." I was sitting in the back seat of his Chevy extended cab, tucked in beside his highly adored golf clubs, and both Mom and Dad were glaring doubtfully at me through the rear-view mirror. In their defence, my track record of being an upstanding human was not excellent.

They had put their butts and, more importantly, their good name on the line for me, and I had better not screw it up...again.

Three months prior, I called my mom from my bachelor apartment in Red Deer, voicing my need for change and adventure.

"I want to move to the island," I said. Anyone who has lived in Canada's prairie provinces knows what "the island" means. It is as though it's the only island in all the world.

"Well, how do you think you're going to do that?" she replied in a familiar non-committal voice.

Her response reminded me of when I was eleven and Janelle and I had big plans to build a go-cart out of my dad's scrap wood in his workshop. We had begun compiling our tools for the project when she met us in the back yard, saying, "Now what the hell are you two doing?"

"We're going to build a go-cart from this junk," I explained.

"Well, you'll never do it. There aren't the right materials here for the job." She laughed joyously at our downtrodden expressions and took a long pull from her cigarette.

"Oh, we'll do it," I mumbled menacingly under my breath. "We'll show you."

As predicted, the go-cart was never brought to fruition. Turns out you need axles, a steering mechanism, and all sorts of things we could not conjure up from the three pieces of lumber and one tricycle wheel we'd gleaned from the shop.

"So? How are you going to go about doing this, Lindsay?" Her voice brought me out of my reverie.

"Well, I thought maybe Dad could call up his grandma there. Maybe I could stay with her until I get on my feet?"

"Oh Lindsay, I don't know about that," Mom said, sounding exhausted with me already.

Looking back, I can understand the hesitation. The last time my mom had vouched for me regarding living quarters, it had not gone well. She was friends with the property manager of one of the local apartment buildings in Sylvan Lake and cautiously put in the right word for me. After four months of late rent payments, moving in four of my closest friends and ultimately still being unable to come up with rent, I crafted a midnight move and fled.

"Can I just talk to Dad, please?" I said, trying to ignore her negativity.

After a considerable amount of bartering and a family dinner where I was forced to lay out my plan of attack for the move, Mom and Dad finally relented.

"Hi, Grandma Jean," Dad yelled into the phone receiver. "It's Dan. Yes, Ruth's son."

"Why is he yelling?" I asked Mom.

"She's deaf. Can't hear a thing over the phone. You will love her, Lindsay. She is one neat old woman." With the understanding that I could stay with her only until September when her sisters would be visiting and require the spare room, I was in.

There are two fundamentals of life that I wholly understand. Cute goes a long way, and always, no matter what, have the ability to gain lawful employment. These lessons have kept me alive and out of severe trouble my entire life.

Two days before I arrived, Grandma Jean had taken the liberty of visiting the manager of the Tim Hortons just up the road. She explained that her great-granddaughter was coming to stay with her, and there wouldn't be any freeloading, so I would need a job as soon as possible. Mom, Dad and I walked in the door to Grandma's apartment after a long and excruciating drive across one and a half provinces, and immediately after introductions, I was told to find a presentable outfit for my interview at the Timmie's the following day. The real question was, what is a presentable outfit for an interview at the prestigious Hortons Institute?

That evening at dinner, Grandma, Mom and Dad reminisced about Dad's childhood while I stewed quietly in the corner. Maybe this whole thing was a mistake. I didn't have it so bad back home. I had my own place, worked a decent job. All my friends were no longer than a twenty-minute drive away. What the hell was I doing here in British Columbia? I was stuck in a two-bedroom condo covered in doilies and throw blankets with a deaf woman who kept calling me Lisa.

"It's Lindsay," Dad would yell into Grandma's good ear. "Lindsay!" Then my dad's piercing eyes caught me, and I remembered his words of warning. *"Don't screw this up, Lindsay."* And I knew there was no going back.

The next morning as I walked in those double swinging doors of the famous coffee house, I was thrown a uniform by an exhausted-looking employee. The shirt was too big, and the pants gave me a cavernous camel toe which I could not hide due to the mandatory shirt-tucking policy. Not even ten minutes in, and I was cursing the eighty-six-year-old woman who had heaved this hell upon me.

"Double Double, NOW!"

"Run those dishes!"

"Write the time on that freshly brewed pot!"

Demands were being hurled at me, and it was overwhelming. It wasn't that I couldn't do the work, but more so because I knew at that very moment my parents were having a glorious time sightseeing the inner harbour and probably out to lunch talking about me and all my shortcomings over mocktails in some swanky café downtown.

I turned my attention to the immediate present. People were lined up and jonesing for their caffeine fix. They all wore angry faces, and I was a little worried about me and my coworkers' well-being.

"Faster, FASTER! You have got to move faster!" My supervisor urged while pouring three large double-doubles, ringing in orders and kicking out a 9 a.m. drunkard simultaneously.

"You haven't actually trained me, though," I began to say.

"Doesn't matter! GO, GO, GO." She was now screaming at me, and my acute anxiety over disappointing people of authority had begun to hammer down. "Whatever, go take a break and collect yourself," she told me while rolling her eyes, wondering how such an idiot had ever graced her employee payroll sheet. I went to the restroom to pull the crotch of my pants out of my labia and put my street clothes back on. I knocked on the manager's door.

"Oh, hello, your shift isn't over yet, is it?" he asked.

"No, I'm sorry, man. I don't think this is going to work out. I'm not cut out for the coffee business."

"Jean will be disappointed when she finds out you haven't finished your shift."

Wait. Was this guy threatening to tell my Grandma on me? I thought about my options for a moment.

"Yeah, well, I'll have to be a disappointment then."

"Oh?" He seemed surprised.

I placed the folded uniform on his desk and said, "Yeah, man." And left.

The decision was a fine one because the next day, I found a housekeeping job at a popular chain hotel. There I'd go on to meet the friends who would carry me through my Victoria days for the following year. I'd also meet one enemy disguised as a handsome boy and see a plethora of drug addicts shooting heroin on the sidewalk just outside the hotel every morning.

Mom and Dad left Grandma Jean's one week later to head back to Alberta. They were secure in knowing I had gained employment. I was nervous to see them go but also incredibly excited.

It turns out eighty-six-year-old roommates are the best kind of roommates. Grandma Jean's quick and hilarious wit combined with a spitfire attitude was not to be compared.

Once, early in our relationship, over a nice quiet dinner, she casually informed me she kept a handsome young man tied up under her bed for when she felt frisky. A piece of mashed potato dropped from my mouth, and she replied, "What? My husband's been dead for years; what's a gal supposed to do?"

You could always bargain on something random coming out of my great-grandmother's mouth when you least expected it. The good times couldn't last forever, though, so after a few months of living in the seniors building with Grandma Jean, I left the nest and moved in with a new friend from work.

Twenty

I am standing on a ladder in the warehouse with an armful of gold acrylic charger plates, trying to determine if we have 500 for an upcoming order.

Although my job description has recently changed, the change was pretty minor. Rather than a simple laundry wench, I'm now the laundry wench who runs this laundry room. It's the perfect sort of promotion for someone like me because the only person I'm in charge of is myself. I just need to make sure our detergents don't run out and all the linens are ready for processing, and looky there, a perfect score on my annual performance review.

The charger plates aren't technically in my department, so they're not really my problem, but I'm in between washes which means I've got a few minutes to spare. I had been browsing our operations board earlier and noted the large order scheduled for the following day, and something in my little hamster brain told me I should do a count on the plates just to be sure we had them available. We should have this information inputted into our inventory system, but unfortunately, we've gone the entire summer with new staff that, unbeknownst to us, have been tossing broken and damaged plates out without marking them down on the inventory sheet. Thus, the counting.

"Lindsay, may I?"

The staff has taken to using this method of approach when asking a question. I deeply loathe it. Typically, when working in a professional kitchen setting, this is how one approaches their superior. (Or anyone if you have a good team.) It's a sign of respect and a great way to avoid unnecessary interruptions when busy.

Our staff, who work closely with catering companies, have taken on this "may I" method and I don't know why it bugs me so much, but it makes my molars ache each time they say it. *Just ask me the damn question, man!* I want to scream but never do.

"Proceed," I say because I never know how to answer the *may I* question. Maybe that's why I hate it so much.

The staff member tells me that our sales manager, Ali, is requesting that I go up front to the showroom. Apparently there is a man with a suitcase who has just walked in and is asking to speak with me. Well, this just got interesting. Maybe a handsome man has come to take me away on a tropical vacation. Perhaps he's a reader of mine and thought to himself *LRB works too hard. She deserves to be beachside, sipping tequila sunrises and looking out on a beautiful ocean while writing her cute little stories.* Sure, the condescension in the guy's tone kind of pisses me off, but I can forgive it because this dude is going to take me to Mexico on his dime.

As I crawl out of my warehouse dungeon, sweaty from ladder climbing and dusty to the touch, Ali introduces me to a large man with impossibly bushy eyebrows.

"This is Lindsay, our laundry specialist," Ali says.

Why can't anyone accept my self-appointed Laundry Wench title? It's not that difficult! As we shake, the man's hands are rough in mine, and I notice his enormous suitcase. Despite the case, I suspect he's not looking to take me abroad.

He, Ali and I sit at the desk, and he labours to lean over to unzip his case on the floor. He then proceeds to slap swatch after swatch of fabric samples on the table, all of which are shedding ruthlessly, leaving fabric shrapnel all over me and the freshly swept floor.

"So what are you good folks in the market for?" His gruff voice and wild eyebrows directly contradict the fact that he's holding a square foot of periwinkle satin in his hands. He reminds me of the mob boss of fine linens. I imagine him reaching up to twirl the tip of his brow in his thick fingers and saying, "I'm gonna make you an offer you can't refuse," while petting a swatch of eucalyptus patterned burlap with the other hand.

It occurs to me that while there aren't a lot of perks that come along with my meagre promotion to laundry room aficionado, this man being here absolutely falls into the benefits category. For you see, this man is a real live travelling salesman.

I was not aware such people existed anymore. My naive brain assumed that if a company wanted to sell their goods country or even worldwide, they would resort to a little thing called the internet. I'm not sure why I am so inwardly excited to be meeting such a business person, but I truly am. I am thrilled that I was deemed the appropriate person to converse with such a character and silently forgive Ali for the whole "laundry specialist" comment earlier. I *am* the laundry specialist here, and I'm starting to like how that sounds.

"These patterns are one of a kind," the travelling linen salesman says while caressing a paisley tablecloth sample. I try to imagine a room full of thirty paisley tablecloths and am overcome with vertigo.

I snap a few photos of his goods and explain that I'll have to discuss with David, who has the final say in such matters. The salesman nods, his eyebrows like great feathery wings swaying gently in his wake.

I return to the warehouse, my mind readying itself to jump back into charger plate counting. I glance at our operations board and begin putting together a to-do list in my brain. We have a busy week coming up and I am going to be ready for it.

Twenty-One

Victoria, BC, is a peaceful city full of lovely tourist attractions and some of the weirdest people you will ever meet. I was one of those weird people.

I had been living there for about six months and was working as a housekeeper. It was a decent gig because I usually walked away at the end of the day with a backpack full of half-drank bottles of any booze you could ask for. Okay, yes, looking back, it's gross AF that I would drink out of bottles that some stranger was drinking from the night before, but do you know what a housekeeper's paid!? Not a lot, dude. Especially after a long day of picking pubes out of drains and checking for stashed hypodermic needles under the pillows on the bed. Yes, that actually happens, and it's pretty rough that a minimum wage worker has to make sure they aren't going to stab themselves with someone's dirty needle while trying to strip a bed. So, yeah, I'd resort to taking the alcoholic riches that the affluent folk would leave behind in their cheap-ass hotel rooms.

I was rooming with my co-worker Becca in a three-bedroom apartment, and this particular day we were stoked at the haul from our hard day's work. A full, unopened bottle of vodka was now safely stored in my backpack, and we were headed home on the bus to get our drink on. Our other roommate, Craig, was due home anytime. He had texted earlier, saying he had a surprise for us when he got home.

That surprise was a pair of handcuffs.

I honestly don't know how he got the cuffs. Craig was a shifty fella, and I learned early on that it was best not to dive too deep into the inner workings of his mysterious life. What I do know is that the cuffs were legit. After playing with them for a while, it became clear that they were not of the plaything variety. These cuffs did not have those tiny levers on the side to release the restraints. You needed a key for freedom, and I supposed that meant they were the real deal.

As we downed shots of vodka (chasing it with cheap fruit punch) and fooled around with our new toy, I thought about how incredible my life was. Here I was, a young lady making her way in the world, cleaning up strangers' pubic hair from nine to five and then living the good life during my fabulous evening hours.

Craig thought it would be funny to cuff Becca and me together. The phone rang while Bec and I were fake crying about being handcuffed to one another. It was a "friend" of Craig's, and he had to run out. Kindly enough, he gave us the key before he left.

With Craig out of the picture, Bec and I figured it would be hilarious to go for a walk in our current state. With the bottle hidden in my oversized handbag, we bused to the Inner Harbour, singing Janis Joplin's Me and Bobby Mcgee. People side-eyed us but didn't pay too much attention. After all, drunk girls were always walking around handcuffed to one another down there—we were not a novelty. The street-famous violin-playing Darth Vader was packing up from a hard day's work and gave us a friendly wave. I realized I had finally become one of the weird Victoria people, and I loved it.

By the time we arrived home, our wrists were beginning to chafe. That's also about the time we made the regrettable realization that we had dropped the key somewhere along our journey. Did we have Darth's number? Could we call him? Maybe it fell in his violin case?

Bec explained that none of these options were viable, so we called Craig instead.

"Do you have a spare key!?" we yelled into the tiny Nokia flip phone. He admitted that he did but was involved with some vital work at the moment and would not be home for a few more hours. That's when the room started spinning. It turns out that drinking an entire twenty-six of vodka on an empty stomach in the space of a few hours while pube-cleanup is still fresh in the mind's eye is not a wise idea.

"Jesus, Linds, don't you dare puke!" Bec yelled in my general direction because she knew me well and could see that famous glint in my eye. The pukey glint. I think it was the word puke that set me off. The word puke is so puke-inducing. It's a pukey word if I've ever heard one.

The vomit was projectile. I'm sure some of it got into Bec's mouth as she screamed at me to stop from her vantage point one foot away. That's the problem when you are handcuffed to a violently ill person—there's nowhere to run. I wanted to stop puking. I did. Puking on someone while you're handcuffed to them is never a good thing. Not advisable. I realized as I sat on the toilet, the hot steam of the shower hitting my hand (the one still cuffed to a person who was now madly trying to rinse my upchuck off her body) that Bec was no longer my roommate; she was now my mortal enemy. Or, I should say, I was now *her* mortal enemy.

I gleaned this information by the way she screamed, "What is wrong with you, Lindsay? Why do you have to puke all of the time? This is so disgusting. Worst roommate ever!" over the sound of the cleansing waters. I hung my head in shame and regretted my easily upsettable tum. Then I puked some more.

When Craig arrived home hours later, Bec and I were passed out on my bedroom floor. Bec had attached a "puke bucket" to me by hanging an old ice cream pail around my neck with a couple of dirty shoelaces in hopes that she would not need to once again feel the bitter sting of her now mortal enemy's vomit sprayed across her once-shiny raven hair.

The puke bucket was a really great idea because I woke up to Craig saying, "Jesus, what the hell happened to you guys? Is that puke in that bucket that's hanging from your neck, Linds?"

It was.

Mine and Bec's friendship never fully recovered because once you have had someone's vodka-flavoured puke in your mouth, you just can't think of them the same way ever again.

I'M NOT THE MANAGER HERE

Twenty-Two

Every morning as I clocked in for work at the hotel, our housekeeping supervisor would give me a list of rooms that needed to be cleaned. Beside each room number the words "Check-out" or "Stay" would be written. The check-outs were pretty straightforward. It meant the guest had checked out of the hotel and it was my job to make that room look as if no one had stayed there before. When setting about cleaning "stays," I'd lightly tap on the still-occupied room doors and ask—while trying to keep my eyes focused on the man's face who is standing at the door, and not his giant penis peeking out of his boxer briefs—if he'd like his room cleaned. I saw so many penises while working at that job.

The memory that sticks out the most, though, was when a very muscular man came dashing out of his room crying with the same sort of hysterical scream reserved for thirteen-year-old girls who have just discovered their crush is calling them on their clear Babysitter's Club phone.

"Yo! Housekeeper, I need you!"

"Oh yeah," I creepily said. "Anything for you." I was but a newly minted twenty-year-old and very horny at this time in my life.

"There's a spider in my room! I need you to kill it!"

Not only was I a horny twenty-year-old, but I was also really into not killing things at that stage in my life. Now? Meh. Back then, though, I was all about peace and love (making). I told the man I'd come in, trap the spider in a paper cup, and bring it outside. He seemed doubtful and didn't understand why I wouldn't just kill the thing but eventually saw that I was unwilling to budge on the deal.

Often, when hotel patrons would stay for long periods in the rooms, they'd end up doing the daily cleans themselves, just asking for new towels or sheets when I'd make my rounds. This man had been staying there for over a week, and I hadn't cleaned his room once.

Upon entering his temporary living quarters, I was hit with the same kind of horror one gets when they are half a mile away from their home, walking the dog, and struck with a debilitating case of stomach cramps. No public bathrooms in sight; they look to the scant bushes with terror in their soul, knowing full well what they must do.

The room was a damn sty.

Pizza boxes littered the floor, with half-eaten crusts milling about upon every counter surface. Skidmarked underwear flung over bedside lamps and doorknobs. The coffee maker was tipped on its side. Do you know how difficult it is to keep those things working? Allowing it to lay on its side, water from the sink pooling around it was going to cause me a world of trouble once trying to clean this place back up to its original glory.

"What. Have. You. Done?" I asked the beautiful muscle man.

"Excuse me?" He replied as if no one had ever scolded him before.

"Do you think that just because you are, like, the hottest guy in the world, you can treat shit that isn't yours like garbage? Do you know how long this is gonna take me to clean up once you're out of here? This is disgusting! How can you live like this?"

It was out of character for me to rage like that, but sometimes, when faced with a situation that seems impossibly dire, the rage just flows out of me without consequence.

"Where the hell is this spider?" I asked angrily.

And that's when I grabbed one of the soggy deteriorating paper cups from beside the toppled-over coffee machine, found the spider, scooped him up and saved him from the pandemonium in which he had been trying to survive. I received a stern talking-to from management the next day at work.

Twenty-Three

As I hid under a large knit throw blanket, high on cocaine, and desperately trying to avoid all the strangers at the party, it occurred to me that I wasn't living my best life. The concept of "your best life" hadn't been invented yet, but I've always been a trailblazer. Three ideas formed in my mind as I fixated on the rough texture of the blanket against my skin. My brain focused with hyper-intensity, and the never-ending loop of these thoughts became my driving force to get my life back on track.

    1. Never do cocaine again.

    2. Get back to Alberta.

    3. Do whatever it takes.

Of course, making a plan of action when you're out of your head on drugs isn't advisable. But sometimes, that's what it takes to get shit done. As the loop intensified, I became more resolved in my quest.

A few weeks prior, I had been moved from the housekeeping department to the laundry room at work. It remains to be seen whether this was a promotion or a demotion. I had been caught sneaking up to the smoking rooms while on shift, for a few puffs throughout the day. The laundry room was beside the manager's office and I think they wanted to keep an eye on me. They couldn't blame me for taking the occasional smoke break while working, though—the job was stressful.

We came across men passed out in bathtubs and vats of lube accompanied by gigantic purple dildos perched nonchalantly on bedside tables. There were countless spiders needing to be saved.

By contrast, the laundry room was a serene place. Yes, there were heaps of ejaculate-drenched bed sheets to be washed, and the occasional crimson tide had sullied a comforter here and there, but I'll take some unwanted bodily fluids over dealing with people any day of the week. In the laundry room, I was free to listen to my music, daydream about the future, and most importantly, start putting some plans into place.

After coming down from my cocaine high the day before, I was back in the safe confines of my laundry room. Although in a much more sober state of mind, I held firm to my resolve that cocaine was the worst, and I'll stick to magic mushrooms, thank you very much. More succinctly, I understood I needed to get back to Alberta. Like yesterday. I wasn't cut out for the clock-less existence of island life. I'm a perpetually nervous human who enjoys the precision of list-making and five-year plans. Granted, I always forget to bring my lists to the grocery store, and I've never once followed through on a five-year plan; it's the journey that counts—that's where I get my kicks, baby.

Alberta, with its oilfield money that I don't endorse but one hundred percent enjoy the spoils of and its fast-paced businessy nature, would help me achieve my ambitions. Alberta: that's home. I started putting out feelers at work about how I might uproot my life once more with exactly zero dollars in my pocket. I'm nothing if not inconspicuous, so I'd slyly ask my coworkers things like, "If you were going to attempt to get to the mainland for free, what kind of sexual favours would you be expecting to perform on the ferry operators to achieve that goal?"

"Oh, Lindsay," they'd say, thinking I was joking.

I'm happy to confess it didn't come to prostitution. After doing a bit more sleuthing, I found out that my friend Ashley's dad was heading to AB to visit family, and I could catch a ride with him. Things like this always happen to me.

I start endlessly obsessing about something I really need, and then the answer appears like magic.

I wish I could say the way things went down was indeed accidental. It would make me seem less conniving. Alas, nothing is an accident in the big scheme of things. Our subconscious drives us to make insane decisions, and without even realizing it, we find ourselves in a cheap motel room lying beside a man who we can only describe as our soulmate.

But the whole soulmate thing comes later. Three weeks before I left Vancouver Island for my home base in Alberta, I was completely sleepless. Sleepless in Victoria, you might say. I was living at my Grandma Jean's again because my roommate Bec and I had flooded our apartment beyond repair when we decided to have an impromptu water fight that went wildly out of control. It's nothing I'm proud of, but it indeed happened. I once again found myself pulling a disappearing act with the magic of a midnight move—foregoing the damage deposit I had coughed up six months prior. In truth, I was happy to get out of that apartment building because a painfully nice man living on the second floor wanted to date me, and I had conflicting feelings about the situation. Dave was a kind thirty-something biker who wanted to treat me like a princess.

We had been on one date where he cooked me a beautiful homemade meal and fawned over the various poems I showed him. He'd stop me in the hallway and tell me how lovely I looked in my grungy blue work scrubs, and he called me m'lady. On paper, the guy was perfect. He was employed, he was kind, and he was interested in everything about me.

He was also roughly 350 pounds. Okay, look, I know how awful this makes me sound. I'm a hypocrite. There have been times in my life when I've clocked in at 220 pounds, and I'm only just over five feet tall. As my Uncle Rob would say, "If you were one inch taller, you'd be square!"

The thing is, I'm nothing if not honest with myself, so I had to ask some important questions when it came to the idea of dating Dave. Questions like, what if I can't find his penis? What if it takes some, for lack of a better phrase, digging around down there? He wants to take me on a bike ride, but can both of us fit on his hog? Doubtful. I may be enticed by his brain, but how long can I be with someone to whom I'm not physically attracted?

I didn't want to be one of those assholes who take one look at a person and say, "Nope, you're too fat for me, my friend," so I gave it the old college try. I hung out with Dave a few times and went on one official date with him. We skipped the awkward small talk and went straight to the deep conversations. We clicked mentally, but as hard as I tried, I couldn't get hot and bothered when imagining myself riding *his* hog.

This all makes me sound incredibly shallow and, of course, I am. But also, ever since then, any time a dude has shut me down because of my weight or general ugliness, I think, *meh, I guess he can't imagine digging around in my pants to find my vagina. No hard feelings.* Pun intended.

I knew it wouldn't be fair to either me or Dave to try to take it any further, so I flooded my apartment as an excuse to get out of that building and never have to see him again. Done and done.

Now I was at Grandma's, and I couldn't sleep. It wasn't because I was thinking about Dave and all the injustices I inflicted upon him. Instead, I was thinking about another man from my past.

I was walking through a flower field. Stone castles peppered the distance, and there, holding my hand, was Jamie. The love of my life. We had met while working at the chicken joint. We had broken up a few years before because we couldn't manage to figure out how to get this dating thing right. We knew we loved each other; we just didn't know *how* to love each other. Then out of nowhere there he was, walking with me through a flower field.

I kept having the dream every night up until I left for Alberta, which was why I ended up being sleepless. I avoided sleeping. I had a lot on my plate, trying to figure out how to get back home sans money. I couldn't deal with the additional trauma of having past loves barge into my REM time.

Once back on the open prairie, the first thing I did was get drunk and call Jamie. See, accidents don't happen.

"Hey, I'm back in town, did you want to meet up at Chef's tonight? Me and Shar are on our way down there right now."

Jamie told me he was busy and couldn't make it. I was bummed but slapped on some lipstick and went out anyway.

The club was the same as it had always been. Same people. Same songs. Same soggy dance floor. I was feeling claustrophobic from the pumping bass and nonsensical jibber jabber being spewed in my ear by a drunk guy who had latched onto me. Then, out of the corner of my eye, I saw him. Wait. Was that him? His mohawk was gone and he looked so presentable! And didn't he say he had other plans tonight?

Years later, Jamie would tell me that he had nonchalantly suggested to his friends they go to Chef's that evening for drinks. His buddies, a team of wannabe rappers and punks, questioned his uncharacteristic proposal since he was not known for having any love for the club scene. When he mumbled, "Well, Lindsay's in town and is going to be there tonight," they laughed at their lovestruck pal and headed my way.

I pushed past drunken bodies and the haze of cigarette smoke to where Jamie was standing. I couldn't help myself. As we closed in on one another, I realized that it was at this moment our story had begun. As it had happened countless times before, I mentally began writing mine and Jamie's love story. In the months to come, I'd write a semi-fictional story that highlighted the exact events of that night, but for now, I wanted to experience every single second that was about to come.

Part Four: Sylvan Lake...Again

Twenty-Four

The midnight air nipped at Beth's skin. She shoved down the very real urge to shriek, "Boy, is it nippily out here!" but she didn't want to be that person anymore. She didn't want to be the kind of girl who yells, "Boy is it nippily out here!" and mean it in all seriousness. But for real, her nipples could slice clean through the CIBC bank vault at this point.

What Beth really wanted was to head back to her hotel room. She greedily yearned for the quiet safety of a warm bath and complimentary slippers. As the last call loomed closer, the city sidewalk was packed tight with bodies and blue-grey clouds of cigarette smoke. Slurred and sloppy voices merrily quarrelled in a drunken stupor as bass reverberated steadily from the club.

Beth was dizzy. Partly from the night's exertion but mostly from the three tequila bombs she downed. She may as well make the most of the rare night out in her hometown. Beth was a smart girl, despite the Cuervo. She knew the longer she lingered, the easier it would be to do something stupid.

Jerald's arm slithered across her shoulders just then. He was so heavily doused in Axe Body Spray that Beth had to work not to recoil from his sudden arrival. Somehow, she had lost her girlfriends, and Jerald had flawlessly moved in to take their place.

"Ready to call it a night?" he asked, placing his jacket over her shoulders.

"Gah, FOMO, you know how it is."

"Oh, not much happens now. You know the drill: pick a pal, find a bed and regret your terrible decisions in the morning."

A giggle crawled out of Beth's throat, which painted a giddy smirk across Jerald's face. He moved closer. She knew what he wanted; his desire was leering at her the way a dog looks at sausage on a dinner plate. She took the slightest step backward and asked Jerald for a light.

Before leaving on her trip home, she had contemplated quitting. She thought that floating onto her old stomping grounds, improved and healthier, would reinvent her into someone exotic, someone glamorous. As much as she had fantasized about living out a real-life rom-com scenario, she knew she didn't have it in her. Sure, she was awkward, but not in the charming, *I'm a blonde-haired supermodel that occasionally snorts when she laughs* sort of way. Beth was more of a, *I'm laughing hysterically at you falling down those stairs and then I let out the loudest, wettest fart of my life,* awkward type. Not exactly leading lady material.

"Oh yeah, sure, babe," Jerald said. There was a rummaging sound as he fished around in his large pockets. *What the hell did he have in there?* Clinking and clanking sounds echoed from his pockets, and Beth wondered what treasures he might be concealing in those deep pouches.

Shit, the T-bombs were doing their magic. Jerald was beginning to look pretty okay to her all of a sudden. He was one of those boys who would always light a cigarette for you. Beth usually hated those sorts of guys. When eventually, they wouldn't be able to find a light, they'd offer to use their lit cigarette with some god-awful euphemism like, "Let me put my hot end to your cold end to make your cold end hot." It was embarrassing for everyone involved. But as she stared into his dopey puppy dog eyes, she mentally shrugged and thought, *meh, why not?*

Jerald had constructed a tent-like arrangement out of a fellow club-goer's jacket, his body, and the body of a drunk man stumbling down the street. Much to his exasperation, the zippo he was using—engraved with his favourite 2Pac lyrics—was not lighting. He continued to make disparaging comments like, "Ugh, dumb lighters, never work when you need them too," and, "This wind is killing me!"

A skin-prickle ran across Beth's forearms. She could feel the unmistakable sensation of someone's gaze on her. But then again, tequila.

She looked around the crowd. People were laughing and flirting and, in one instance, basically fucking. Others were engrossed in tales about what they might do to save the planet one day. How they could run a country better than what's his name. Who was having an affair with whom? These sidewalk people were in deep-conversation mode. They were solving the world's problems one drunken proclamation at a time. And the feeling that someone was observing her would not lessen.

Then, as if Moses himself appeared to perform a humble miracle on Lakeshore Drive, the sea of humans split, leaving Beth exposed on that boozy city sidewalk. The man standing before her slung buckshot butterflies into her gut. His hair was different, cut clean and close to his scalp. His eyes were as blue and old as they had always been. As their gaze met, he looked to the ground but not without a grin cracking open his face.

Beth's body began to move toward him. *What the hell was she doing?* Jerald's jacket dropped to the ground, and the flame from the 2pac lighter went out. Maybe her rom-com dreams were coming true after all.

Two years stretched between Beth and Lance. Two years of memories dwindled by time and distance. Two years of scrounging together titbits of information from mutual friends about Lance's life. Who he was seeing. Where he was working. She cobbled together scraps of information about him the way a kidnapper scrapbooks a ransom note.

He never mentioned her, friends would say awkwardly after she finally got up the nerve to ask. Although this gulled her endlessly, it wasn't surprising. He never allowed his emotions to escape. It was too messy. It was too "Beth."

Her chest erupted in tenderness as she saw nothing but this man she had loved for years and had been creepily dreaming about for weeks. She wanted to say something coy to show him how much she had matured in their time apart, how cool and confident she was now.

Her hands moved toward him like she was a demented zombie looking for brain Wellington. *What the hell am I doing?* She wondered feverishly as her hands continued on their frenzied quest. *Braiiiins. What if he was here with someone? What if he had a girlfriend? What if he wanted nothing to do with her?*

None of it mattered. The fear was gone.

Beth opened her mouth to say something. All she needed was a simple greeting to dribble out from between her watering lips. It seemed that entire armies were stopping the words from coming forth. The guy was always leaving her speechless.

Years from now, when they were settled down with a family, he would still be doing it. As their children galloped by on hardwood floors with bare feet and sticky faces, he would reach over and place his hand on her leg, sending a shock of electricity up her spine. Reminding her how one-of-a-kind their life had been together.

Her hands reached toward the man that she could spend millennia with, and she knew what this meant for her life. Her course had shifted. He reached to her with a similar brain-seeking posture and pulled her close. He moved in to kiss her; this time, she took the offer eagerly.

Romcom magic.

The sidewalk people continued with their drunken parleys, none the wiser to the history which was taking place right in front of them.

Twenty-Five

Susie has a way of looking at me that kills every defence mechanism I've worked so hard to construct these past 37 years. She asks me what's wrong and I tell her nothing, then she stares not into my soul but engulfs it, making me totally aware she is basically a ninja when it comes to brain health.

"No, seriously, why are you so stressed out right now?" She asks because I'm currently having a complete emotional breakdown due to all of the overflowing laundry bins filling the warehouse. It's been a busy week and the overwhelm is getting to me. Being in the laundry room isn't providing me with the joy it usually does. Being here reminds me of that feeling you get when you're scarfing down perogies and sausages and realize, a split second too late, that you've been eating way too fast and now a clump of perogy-sausage is regrettably stuck at the bottom of your food chute and you're all like, "Okay. This is it. This is how I die."

Death by a thousand poorly chewed bites of sausage. Death by a thousand unfinishable laundry room tasks.

"I just don't know how to do this anymore," I blurt. "The detergent isn't getting any of the grease stains out of the napkins, I've been asking the boys to put those chair covers away for days now, I have no idea how to keep track of all the disappearing linens, and that sewer smell is worse than ever!"

"Is that really what's bothering you, Lindsay?" Susie doesn't say this in a condescending way, but my knee jerk reaction to scream at her persists anyway. Why does kindness put me on edge so much? I don't scream at Susie, though, because she's the last person I'd want to hurt. Instead, I look deep into my brain while digging deep into a bin of beer-soaked kitchen rags and realize the problem.

"What I really want is to write," I say. "This job is taking up so much of my mental and emotional real estate there's nothing left by the time I get home and sit down at my computer."

I confess this to Susie in a tone that would make me want to puke in my mouth, if I heard it coming out of someone else's mouth. 'Oh for Christ's sake, shit or get off the pot,' I'd probably yell at them. I have little tolerance for whining and yet, here I am whining.

Susie is a much better human than me so she doesn't tell me to shit or get off the pot. Instead, she simply says, "Lindsay, what are you talking about? You are a writer. Writing is your first job. This is just the secondary job."

Twenty-Six

I've endured my share of bad employers, but the worst was when I was newly pregnant with my son, Lars. I was once again housekeeping at a run-down motel in my hometown. I was already fired up about this place because the management refused to move me to the front desk when I asked. I wasn't above housekeeping but I was a bit neurotic as a preggo and worried that the flipping of mattresses and inhaling all the heavy cleaners might do my little fetus harm. The management told me I wasn't front desk material. I don't know what they considered "front desk material" considering their squalid living quarters were clearly visible behind the front desk.

Then, the manager of this motel pulled a Trump and literally grabbed me by the pussy.

While watching me clean rooms—an exercise he laboured at whenever possible—he began telling me a story. He walked over to where I was vacuuming and stood uncomfortably close. Then he asked, "Do you mind?"

Do I mind what? I wondered. I had no idea what he was referring to. A display of physical contact didn't seem to pertain to his tale about golfing with his buddies, so I shrugged and said, "Um, okay?" He then went on to tell me how a friend of his grabbed a waitress in that general vicinity. For some awful reason, he thought I needed a visual "like this" and proceeded to do the same thing to me.

I was devastated. It was sickening how nonchalant he made the entire thing. *Nothing to see here,* he seemed to be saying, without saying, *just clutching this young pregnant woman's snatch.*

The feeling of having an almost-stranger touch me unexpectedly and in such an intimate place was so viscerally uncomfortable I gasped and tears welled immediately in my eyes. The manager made eye contact with me for a split second and then stepped back, releasing his, er, grip and held his hands up, palms facing me. As if to say, "Hey, you okayed this, bitch." My stomach clenched and I didn't have the words to say anything at all. I went back to vacuuming the floor.

I still feel ashamed that I put myself in that position. I feel ashamed that I endangered myself. I feel ashamed that I didn't spray the asshole in the face with industrial cleaner and storm straight out of that motel room and over to the cop shop. I feel ashamed of it all. No wonder women have difficulty coming forward about these things—our shame quotient is too damn high. The sad truth is, I was under the ill-informed impression that because he had asked and I had said "okay," I was in the wrong.

I wish I would have had a wise older woman on my side back then who would have said the words, "Don't let anyone fool you into thinking they can grab your pussy. It's never okay to have someone grab your pussy unless you are naked in bed with them and explicitly ask them to grab your pussy. No human being alive has the right to grab your dang pussy."

Unfortunately at that time, I had no women like this in my life.

I never want any person I care about to have to go through something so stupid and demoralizing and just plain awful so despite being the kind of person who has a very difficult time saying "pussy" in any context other than the willow variety, I say those exact lines to all the young women I know. And yes, it gets weird.

I left that job after a few months when I was overlooked for the front desk position yet again. For the remainder of my pregnancy, I worked as a prep cook in a bar—which ended up being loads safer and more pleasant than the housekeeping gig.

Twenty-Seven

When I was seven months preggers with my son, I weighed approximately the same as a narwhal. I was sweaty all the time and slick to the touch, mimicking the famed unicorn of the sea. Short of having a long, sharp horn on my head, I was quite reminiscent of this particular sea creature — a marvel to look at from afar, but nobody wanted to get too close for fear I might turn on them.

While all this corpulence was going on, I was working as a prep cook at a local pub.

"Load me up with a large plate of poutine. Extra curds, please!" I'd say heartily to the cook while on my second lunch break of the day. Working at a greasy bar while having all sorts of weird pregnancy cravings was not a great thing for my health.

My chef, Betsy, was a strange woman. One minute, she'd be bragging about the fact that she still owned the same gym socks she had in high school and in the next breath, she was crying because customers weren't complimenting her take on the classic BLT (she added pickles).

Another weird thing about Betsy: she was constantly asking people to guess her age. She might meet someone for a whole of three minutes and was already saying her classic line, "Now, I want you to guess how old I am? I bet you can't do it!"

Of course, the grocery delivery man, the health inspector, or whoever was unlucky enough to come into contact with this awkward inquiry would reply, "Oh. I'd rather not. I've got a lot of work to do here." But Betsy was persistent.

"Come on, just throw me a bone here—guess my age! Guess it!"

I'm not saying all line cooks are haggard, but the job does tend to cast a veil of exhaustion over one's previous unblemished features. Simmering away in above-average temperatures on the line and the stress of dealing with sobbing servers due to hangry customers does not bode well for a stress-free work environment. Chefing is the kind of career where you don't get paid nearly enough for the bullshit that constantly surrounds you.

So yes, sometimes cooks age a bit faster than other people. This is why whenever Betsy would strong-arm people into guessing her age, she'd always come away pouting.

They would always guess that she was at least a few years older than she was.

Why would anyone want a stranger to guess their age? Are these people delusional? Thinking, ah yes, I look so young and fresh I want to hear about it from random strangers. Everyone I encounter must know that I look younger than my age; hence, I will force them to guess my age and then laugh at their stupid, stupid faces when they get it wrong.

And they would get it wrong in Betsy's case. So direly wrong.

There I'd be, stuck consoling the woman while the apologetic bread guy brought in racks of Texas toast. Betsy scream-swearing that we were going to have to get a new bread guy because this fucker was an asshole! Betsy never learned her lesson when asking strangers to guess her age. That is until I decided to teach her a lesson.

A repair person had come in to fix the dishwasher which was on the fritz. Betsy, being Betsy, started in on him, asking how old he reckoned she was. Just as that familiar twitch of "this is a trap, man" crossed over this guy's face, I turned to Bets and said, "Hey! Since we're playing the numbers game, how about this one..." I paused.

While looking both Betsy and the repair guy in the eyes for much longer than acceptable, I dropped the bomb, "How much do you think I *weigh*."

Immediate agony crossed their petrified faces.

The repair guy looked at Betsy with bewilderment. It was clear he was frantically searching for an escape route and hadn't yet found the proverbial exit sign. Betsy stared back at him, looking uncomfortable but did not break eye contact because that was just the kind of human Betsy was. Finally the repair guy said, "I need to go get a part from my van," and straight-up ran away.

Betsy dared to be angry with me for putting her and the repairman in such an awkward position.

I wanted to retort, "That's what you've been doing all along," but realized it was hopeless.

It seemed that guessing an obese person's weight was more offensive than guessing an old person's age. In the end, my plan worked perfectly. I never again witnessed Betsy corner a perfect stranger in an attempt to get some sort of backward compliment out of them. Instead, she kept making me those cheesy poutines and telling me cringy tales about her ancient gym socks.

And in the strange world that is the restaurant biz, you can't really ask for much better than that.

Twenty-Eight

I don't know when my disinterest for children who are not mine kicked in. It was somewhere around the time my kids started developing personalities, and I realized they are so much cooler than anyone else in the entire world.

This time also coincides with my adoption of strident feminism and the realization that I don't have to pretend to love all children just because I was born with ovaries.

But before all these incredible revelations, I was told I should take a job in childcare. It was a time when I was at a loss about what to do. All while the looming worry of "the future" crept up on me. I knew I was supposed to be making some sort of plan. All my friends were getting real jobs, so I figured I should too.

Granted, I already had a baby, but I've never been one to do things in the expected order.

I had worked at a daycare about five years before, but that only lasted a few weeks after I accidentally locked a kid in a bathroom and forgot about him there. I know it doesn't sound great when I talk about my disgust for kids, and then I reveal I once locked one in a bathroom.

The two things are entirely unrelated.

And it wasn't even me who locked him in there. That little dummy locked himself in the bathroom, and I simply forgot he was there. I took the other kids outside to play and then, about twenty minutes later, realized we were down a head and ran back inside to find the boy happily playing with toilet water to keep his brain occupied while enduring his solitary confinement.

Everyone was fine.

Unfortunately, my supervisor and the boy's parents didn't have the same thoughts, and I was written up. After realizing that shit was real when looking after kids, I quit because that was too much responsibility for me. Now, five years later, I was about to go at it again.

This time it would be different, I told myself. Rather than preschool-aged kids, I'd be in charge of six to ten-year-olds, a much easier age range I figured.

I was wrong. Oh, so very wrong.

The problem with school-aged kids is that they find their distinct personalities at this age. Until now, they were a mix of their parent's ideals and idiosyncrasies. Then, as soon as they are allowed the freedom of six whole hours parent-free, that tiny shell begins to crack open, and an entirely new little monster emerges.

Sometimes these monsters are sweet or surprisingly funny with astute observations about the world around them—these are the types of children I will tolerate with what passes as gracious amusement. I'm lucky in the sense that to this day, my kids have been wise in their selection of friends, and they all seem to fall under this category.

More often, the shell cracks and a real live gargoyle appears out of nowhere. Whether it's privilege, rudeness, cockiness, or all the above, the qualities these kids carry with pride make you want to wring their little necks.

How on earth do you think it's appropriate to tell me that I waddle when I walk? I'd think after an eleven-year-old said these exact words to me after my first shift at the after-school program.

"All I'm asking is that you take your muddy boots off before entering the gym!" My voice would quiver as I tried to remain calm while reasoning with a belligerent eight-year-old with pigtails. The job, I realized, was a nightmare, and I was only three hours into my first shift.

People don't work in childcare because of the easy schedule or the load of money you make, and I was no different. There certainly isn't a ton of money in the after-school programs funded by the Alberta government, so I was making minimum wage while ensuring the gargoyles didn't kill themselves while their parents were working.

The program ran out of an elementary school classroom. Any kids who didn't have after-school care would make their way to the classroom as soon as that 3 p.m. bell rang, and there they'd play until a parent could pick them up.

We'd craft and read and put on plays and do all the things that are fun to do with kids if you're doing them with the right kind of kids. And sometimes, the other caregivers and I would get lucky, and it would only be the right kind of kids that showed up that day.

Those were the greatest shifts, ones where we didn't have to negotiate with a nine-year-old on why he couldn't paint all over the classroom walls. "Put the paintbrush down, and I'll let you grab a treat from the treasure box," we'd say as if speaking to an overworked circus monkey wielding a blowtorch.

Oh, how we abused the existence of the treasure box. It was a small chest filled with candy and dollar store toys meant for positive reinforcement when kids were behaving. Instead, in those early days of caregiving, we bribed the shit out of those little shits, and to be honest, it worked out well for all parties involved.

So yes, I didn't stay for the pay or, unlike most of my coworkers, the kids; instead it was the convenience of the job that kept me there for so long. The school was only a five-minute walk from my house, which was a definite bonus. Not to mention, it got people off my back.

The number of times I've taken a shitty job just to get people to stop asking me, "So what about your future, Lindsay," is insane.

What about, "I'm going to be a famous writer," do these people not understand?!

I stayed at the childcare place for a little over three years. Mostly it was part-time/casual work because about a year in, I gave birth to a Sophie-kid and realized that working in childcare to pay for childcare was redundant.

I had been considering quitting for some time but hadn't gotten around to it yet. Then one day, as I sat in a large circle of kids on a hard gymnasium floor, a sweet-looking blond girl with an evil grin looked directly into my soul and said, "Those earrings you're wearing look like they're from the dollar store."

"Um, these earrings are super old and fancy. My mother-in-law gave them to me, and they were her mom's from England, thank you very much," I said, trying to match the small child's level of bitchiness.

"Definitely from the dollar store," she replied, laughing.

"Look, you little shit, I do buy my earrings from the dollar store, but these ones aren't from there, okay. And what the hell is it your business anyways where my earrings come from?" I angrily whispered so none of the other caregivers would hear.

She was much more skilled at the art of arguing than I was because the rage I felt when she replied with a shrug and a flip of her hair was so intense, I realized then and there that it was probably best to throw in the towel with this childcare thing once and for all.

Twenty-Nine

I've always been a little bit magic. Not like, I'm-getting-a-letter-from-Hogwarts magic, but the sort of magic that manifests deep within the soul. I visualize things, and within weeks or months, there they are, sitting in front of me.

Of course, the magic doesn't work when I try to conjure up Channing Tatum in boxer briefs and a big, hard package of rock candy for me to gnaw on. No, the universe does not see these fantasies fit to bestow on me.

When I was young, the things I tried to bring to fruition with my magic abilities always had to do with love and romance. Oh my stars, was I ever into love and romance in those formative years. The first time I realized these fantasies were coming true was when I went on a particularly obsessive daydreaming kick while living in Victoria and thinking about an old flame with whom I still loved years after our breakup.

Within weeks, I ended up running back to my hometown and into the guy at one of our hometown bars. Then we accidentally got pregnant, married, and popped out another kid a few years later. *Magic!*

Suddenly I was a new mother at twenty-three, with two very small humans to look after and it became apparent that I needed something else in my life that was just for me. Mothers are supposed to be these endlessly giving creatures who sacrifice until they are mere shells of the people they were before taking on the responsibilities of other human lives. But the truth is, I'm not that selfless.

I would imagine a life stretched far ahead of me that consisted solely of these two babes, and it gave me chills. I worried motherhood would soak up every ounce of Lindsayness I had as I grew dull with the minutiae of bedtime routines and playdates with fellow moms who were also witnessing their very essence flitting away. I worried that the label of Mom would become my only defining characteristic.

Not to mention, what would I do once the kids hit adulthood? Or worse yet, teendom. I didn't know much about children, but I did know that between the ages of thirteen and twenty-one, kids have little-to-no use for the grownups who brought them into this world. They have bigger, more important things going on. They are smarter than some idiot parent. They don't have time to waste on their pathetic old mother. I knew this because it hadn't been long since I was in that stage myself.

"I think you should try out this blogging thing," Janelle said one day while we were having our daily best friend phone chat.

"What's blogging?" I asked, regretting that I was never in-the-know when it came to the newest fads.

"I dunno, people write stories on the internet. Most of them are funny and a lot of moms are doing it. They write about raising kids. Then bored and slightly depressed mothers read it. I bet you could do that." This is Janelle all over. She has endless encouragement for the people she loves. I wasn't convinced.

I doubted anyone would want to read stories about my life. I couldn't imagine admitting to readers about that one time Lars kept purposefully dripping his juice cup on my freshly washed floor, and finally screaming, "Stop it, you little shit weasel!"

But I loved my two little shit weasels. I took great pride in the interesting humans they were becoming. I knew I'd forever put them first—but in order to put your children first, you must create something to put them ahead of. I thought about Janelle's proposal for a week, and then one late night, when I couldn't fall asleep, I tiptoed out to the living room and fired up the computer.

If I didn't write, I knew I'd become some crazy-ass clingfilm mother who hovered over my children's every move. I'd stalk them at high school parties by dressing up as a student, and when word got out that the lunatic forty-year-old dressed in bell bottoms and a flower power tee was Lars and Sophie's mom, their social life would be ruined. I couldn't let that happen to my darling little ones.

I started the blog. I wanted to show my children that having goals and passion in life is an integral part of the human experience.

The blog's name was The Blogging Mama, and I wrote about my life as a stay-at-home mom. It wasn't anything new. As Janelle had mentioned, pretty much any remotely funny mother with an inclination for the written word was doing the same thing back in 2011. I had always enjoyed writing, so it seemed the logical next step. I needed something new and exciting in my life. Something that would ward off the functional depression that being a lonely stay-at-home mom was threatening to provide.

A year after starting the blog, I developed a segment called Helen the Housewife. A friend of mine was getting her photography business off the ground and asked if I wanted a free session. Kismet! This would be perfect. I could use the photos to accompany jokes that satirize a bored housewife's life.

In today's culture, someone would have been deeply offended by those articles. In the glory days of 2011, they landed me a job writing for a local newspaper. I found an online ad calling for writers to craft family-style articles for the Red Deer Advocate's blog. Being the ever-optimist I was back then, I sent in my writing resume (literally my blog's web address) and promptly forgot about the entire thing.

An editor named Leo emailed me a few weeks later, letting me know he loved my Helen the Housewife series on The Blogging Mama and would like to share it on the Advocate's website. Of course, there was no pay, but who cared? I was blogging for free anyway, so any extra mentions meant more eyeballs on my work.

For about three months, Leo reposted my stories to The Red Deer Advocate page, and I giddily bragged to random people on the street that I was an official blogger for a real-life newspaper. Then the thing happened. The thing that gave me the kind of confidence in my writing that is probably not warranted but spurred me on in those early years. Leo asked me to go steady.

Well, er, not me. He asked my writing to go steady with the newspaper. The Advocate offered me a weekly column in the family section of the paper. The pay was thirty dollars a week, which at the time felt amazing because I had never been paid to write a damn thing. Thirty dollars for a 600-word article? Um, yes please! I named the column Me Plus Three and continued writing stories about the life and times of Jamie, the kids, and myself.

I often wondered how I landed the job in the months and years that followed. I hadn't gone to school for writing. I was a stay-at-home mom with atrocious spelling and a weird sense of humour. The oddity of the opportunity was not lost on me. Then I remembered I was magic. It's always been like this. Obsess for long enough, and eventually, something resembling your fantasy will come true. I wanted to be a writer. I wanted to make people laugh. I wanted to do something that would allow me to be at home with my kids but gave me my own identity.

Presto chango, I became a mommy blogger!

After my big writing break, I keep my magical daydreaming to work-related stuff. There's a fundamental reason for this. I always have room to move on to bigger and better things career-wise because, in a financial sense, I'm broke. But I can't risk the seemingly innocent act of fantasizing about a romance with anyone but my husband because the magic has only been getting more potent in my elder years. It seems that if I even spend, say, ten to seventeen hours consecutively obsessing over a reasonable thought, that thought will become a reality within weeks of the fantasy.

So obviously, I must keep my daydreaming of wild sex with strangers to a minimum because who knows how strong this thing will get and then I'd be stuck in a very awkward love triangle situation and Jamie and I have never talked about if he's into that sort of thing or not.

Thirty

As was the case most mornings back then, I woke up next to a massive wet spot in bed beside me. I spotted a fleece Scooby Doo blanket crumpled next to the crime scene, which revealed the perpetrator of the offence. It seemed four-year-old Lars had shuffled into my bedroom sometime during the night, crawled into bed beside me to let flow and then retreated to his room to sleep in a pee-free sanctuary. I sighed, pulled myself out of bed, and rallied my tired, urine-soaked body.

When you're a mother of two kids under four, diamonds are not a girl's best friend—coffee is. Jamie was due to wake up anytime as he was working the morning shift at one of the local restaurants in town. Sophie bellowed a "Mama!" from her room, and I went to greet the two-year-old. Sophie was an extraordinarily easy baby. Most days, she'd sit in the living room watching her big brother play with his Thomas the Train figurines in front of the TV playing the corresponding show.

I greeted my girl and plopped her down in her activity center in the living room. Lars had awoken by this point, and when I confronted him about my sodden bed, he shrugged his shoulders and played dumb. He's always been a smart kid.

The morning progressed as most mornings did back then. I finished an article I was writing for the Red Deer Advocate, kissed Jamie as he left for work, and called Janelle for our regular morning coffee chat. As I animatedly retold the story about waking up in a puddle of pee to my child-free friend, I began to smell something suspicious. It's the kind of stench that only parents are well versed in. I told Janelle I would have to let her go and cautiously entered the living room.

There before me was a sight of horrific proportions. Sophie had somehow escaped the activity center—I'm assuming she had an accomplice named Lars—and she was now sitting naked beneath the computer desk. I found her quickly enough since she had decided to remove her shit-filled diaper and proceed to fingerpaint with the contents all over our living room. Brown sludgy poo-prints peppered the light blue carpeting. A snail trail of fecal matter ran from her activity center to her current location under the desk. Oh, the horror.

"What happened?" I screamed to no one in particular.

This alerted Lars, my ever-studious boy, to loom nearer and begin speaking in tongues about the devastation his kid sister had caused.

"Mama, Sop pooed eddywhere!" The rest of his sentence was indecipherable.

I wanted to scream, "No shit, Sherlock!" but understood somewhere deep in my quickly darkening soul the inappropriateness of such a comment. So instead, I did as mothers the world over have done, and I cleaned that shit up with grace and dignity. Quietly muttering, "This is fucking bullshit. Gawd damn kids and their gawd damn messes!" the entire time.

The doorbell rang amid the craptastrophe, and as I answered it, I realized too late there was a streak of feces smeared across my fluorescent yellow sweater.

It was a small girl selling chocolate-covered almonds for some kind of fundraising project. *Okay. Now we were getting somewhere,* I thought. I could use a little pick-me-up. The girl stared at the strange woman before her. A woman with a naked, shit-stained baby in her arms. A woman with a skidmark that could fill the depths of hell smudged across her fluorescent yellow sweatshirt. A woman with a watery-eyed gaze locked on those chocolate-covered almonds with yearning.

I know in my heart of hearts the small child noted the shit streak immediately. A frazzled woman, clad in a sweater brighter than the sun, with a large swath of green-brown baby BM smeared lovingly across her chest—how could even the most unobservant person miss such a spectacle?

We made our trade, though, because chocolate is life. I will forever hold that little girl in my heart for the kindness she demonstrated that day. How easy it would have been for her to run away crying about the horrific things she witnessed just inside the door of my poop-strewn home.

With a box of chocolate-covered almonds grasped tightly in my claws, I sank down on the other side of the door and began to cry. Was I cut out for this? I had never really enjoyed the company of children, so what made me think my children would be any different? Streams of Lashblast mascara painted tiny black rivers of degradation down my face. I sobbed into my stool-soaked hands and envisioned the grim future of child-rearing.

"Mama," Sophie said, standing before me and looking deep into my tear-filled eyes. She lifted her hand, one that still smelled unbearably of poo, and rubbed my face lovingly. Lars came over then and hugged me. Together I sat with these disgusting little humans, whom I loved so intensely it hurt. And I knew with absolute resolve I'd clean up an eternity worth poo in exchange for getting to be their mother.

Meanwhile, Jamie was restless. After graduating from trade school and receiving his Red Seal in cooking, he found work as a chef in many of the local bars and restaurants in Sylvan Lake. He even went on to land a position managing the kitchen at our town's Golf and Country Club, which shows that, unlike me, Jamie has always had an unrelenting drive to move upwards in his profession.

Any ambitious chef can tell you that there comes a point when you tire of cooking up someone else's dreams. So one day, he came home from work and said, "What would you say about opening a sandwich shop with me?"

Thirty-One

"Me and Susie almost killed ourselves trying to scale and then dismantle the Everest of linen boxes your takedown crew left us last night." My words are sharp and dripping with frustration. There's a familiar lump forming at the base of my throat, and I know that the tears are not far behind. I'm not frustrated with David directly, but that's who I'm taking my anger out on.

Over the past few months, the staff has noticed a shift in the warehouse and it seems that a few of them do not like it. Susie and I are taking on extra responsibility here and there until David can find a warehouse manager. The business is growing, and he's finding it nearly impossible to juggle business meetings, customer consultations, bookwork, and managing the warehouse staff with the recent upsurge in clientele. He needs a warehouse manager.

"I told them to unstack those bins last night. They didn't?" David asks.

"They sure didn't. Do you know how difficult it is for us to lift twenty pounds of used linens off the top of an eight foot tall tower of bins? I'm like five foot nothing!" I'm not sure if it's the situation at hand or the fact that I've always been a little self-conscious of my stumpy stature, but it is at this moment the tears spill over. I want to stop the tears, but I'm helpless to shove them back into my now sopping wet sockets. I should at least turn away so my boss doesn't have to witness this pathetic display of humanness.

"I just feel so disrespected, David. They laugh at me when I ask them to do their jobs, for Christ's sake. I don't want to be responsible for this place. I'm just a laundry wench, remember?"

It is my bad luck that I tend to ramble when stressed. Well, ramble and cry. David is uncomfortable. I can tell by the hurt look on his face and his awkward posture—he has no idea what to do with me right now.

All I can say is, "Find a manager, soon."

Part 5: Lethbridge

Thirty-Two

There is an empty strip mall bay nestled between a pizza place and a head shop. It isn't much to look at because the walls are a piercing white, almost headache-inducing. There is no power running to the place. When the property manager, who is weathered and long-haired, shows the young couple around, the deeper into the bay they explore, the darker it gets.

This husband-and-wife team has dreams in their eyes. They have moved to this new city with their young family in hopes of creating something big. Eddies of possibility twirl through high ceilings and out toward a busy midday street. Their hearts are puttering because without exchanging words, they both know they have found the space.

The manager brings the two into the basement, which is unfinished and smells earthy. He pops on a flashlight, and for a brief moment, the woman wonders if this was a ploy to murder them in this creepy abandoned-looking hole in the floor. Due to an unfortunate core memory having to do with potato storage, the woman hates cellars. But she says nothing because she is here to support her husband. The couple follows the strange old hippy into the unlit basement.

The bay is perfect, and the price is right. They agree then and there that this will be the space to start their new business venture. Hands are shaken. Smiles had by everyone.

The sandwich shop is born.

Thirty-Three

Over the three years we owned the Hot Wire Panini, our most frequently asked question was, "Do you guys own this sandwich shop?" closely followed with, "Wow, that's awesome, you're married then?" and finally, "Don't you guys drive each other nuts?"

We'd tell them we hate each other and are just in this thing for the money. Mom and Pop shop owners are notoriously lucrative if you didn't know. Often, when asked if we were married, we'd look bewildered and say, "Um no, we're brother and sister," then Jamie would grab my ass while maintaining a stern amount of eye contact with our current company.

Once we had explained that we were pulling their leg and, yes, we are a husband-and-wife team, the response was always the same: "I'd never be able to work with my wife/husband. I'd kill them!" We'd laugh noncommittally and nod, telling them, "Oh boy, it's come close to that before!" Jamie might mime-strangle me, causing me to pretend to fall down dead. Jamie then would scream, "You killed her!" and that was my cue to spring back up from the floor and yell, "Gotcha!" with jazz hands.

As I am writing this, it all seems a bit much. But this line of questioning could be a bit much. Of course it's not easy working with your spouse. It's not easy working with a stranger or a best friend or a sibling. It's not easy working with

I'M NOT THE MANAGER HERE 129

anyone because every person has a distinct way of doing things. Isn't that the purpose of kindergarten? To learn how to play well with others.

When we first began setting up The Hot Wire, I worried about so many things. Mostly though, would there be a power struggle between me and my husband? Well, not really, because he knew everything about the food and beverage industry, and I knew nothing. That determined our roles in the company pretty darn quickly. Although, most of the time, I would still pretend to be the boss, and he'd play along because he is a goddamn saint.

He often called me "Boss," and I would roll my eyes but quietly tuck away a smile because I knew he did this to make me feel good about my place at our business. It's not all cutesy name-calling and ass-grabbing when it comes to spouses working together. There were days when we'd had enough of each other. When one of us had said or done something to piss the other off, we avoided each other the way you avoid stank on a musty towel. There we'd be, Jamie sitting on one side of the restaurant, me on the other, drinking our coffee and purposefully not acknowledging the other's presence.

We fought a lot while owning the business. Sometimes we'd be in the middle of the mother of all domestic disputes when a customer would approach the door, and we'd turn it off like a magic button had switched off the aggressive part of our brains. The person walking in was none the wiser because that's what the customer service industry is all about. You pretend to play nice in order to fill up that cash register.

Our business didn't care about hurt feelings or disagreements. It only knew good service. Relationships and personal tribulations became secondary during regular business hours. This is the mom-and-pop shop motto.

I'd often be angry at Jamie and sulking when I realized I needed to speak with him about something business-related. Maybe it was our next sandwich special or something to do with the bookkeeping. 99.9% of me wanted to ignore the issue and continue giving him the silent treatment. Because, long story short, I'm a stubborn asshole. But I knew that wasn't an option when it came to our business. So, I would deflate my ego and carry on with professional matters.

Jamie and I were friends before we dated. We disagree on almost everything. We argue over the small details. We drive each other crazy most of the time with our vastly differing opinions on topics from politics to poetry. He loves Snorri Sturluson, and I can't even get through one damn page of Heimskringla because it's a damn tome. He laughs at spoken word poetry, the only kind I can write. We still make time to listen to one another's opinions though. We respect each other regardless of everything; that's how we made our business work.

You could say my husband and I are friends with benefits. However, our *benefits* far exceed the sexual favours of the popular idiom (although that's nothing to shake a stick at). We are fortunate enough to have the benefit of choosing our own path. We make decisions regarding money, business, family, children, and life together. We hold each other up in times of stress, and we celebrate as one in times of victory.

Working together had its trials, but the trials seemed minuscule compared to the triumphs. Sometimes, it felt as though it was too much; sometimes, we worried we'd taken on more than we could chew. But we moved through those rough patches together and kept on growing.

Plus, a morning quickie in the office—despite it being an awkwardly positioned affair—made for an invigorating way to begin the workday.

Thirty-Four

When Steve came into our lives, he reminded me of a fish flopping around on hot cement. Sure, he was vaguely offensive and sort of smelly, but he was desperately pleading for help, so we agreed to give him a moment of our time.

When first opening the shop, we were always on the lookout for great deals. With having to bring in fresh products weekly, this became a job in and of itself. We found that as far as our primary food needs went, buying the bulk ingredients (flour, sugar, butter, milk, etc.) and making our bread and pastry products from scratch was the most cost-efficient method.

Our biggest problem was where to find affordable paper products: paper towels, sandwich boxes, napkins, and the like. It seemed that each provider we found was either overpriced or providing us with a grossly inadequate product.

Here enters Steve.

Our first summer in operation was slow, which meant finding affordable products was the priority. Steve was short and plump with a high-pitched voice that stayed with a person long after he had left the room.

"Is the owner here, little lady?" Steve spoke in my general direction while simultaneously never acknowledging me.

"You're looking at her," I replied, and the immediate disappointment on Steve's face was long and lasting. After several moments of his melancholy mug staring at me blankly, I began to grow uncomfortable.

I didn't know Steve yet, so I was unaware that we were still living in the 1950s and he was disappointed there wasn't a man to conduct his business with. Instead, I assumed he was feeble of mind or perhaps undergoing some sort of minor stroke, paralyzing his face in this horrified state.

"Can I help you with something, sir?" I spoke slowly and quietly so as not to startle him.

"Is...is it just you who owns this restaurant?" He began looking behind the counter as though he might find someone crouching between my legs, waiting to pounce.

"Gotcha, friend; of course it's not only a woman running an outstanding business such as this!" the man in hiding might yell upon meeting Steve's eyes.

"My husband and I run the shop."

Steve let out an audible sigh. "Oh, well, where is he?"

"Excuse me?" I began counting silently in my brain. I have found that this helps me quiet the rage monster I inherited from my father when faced with moments of frustration. "He's not here right now, but I'd be happy to help you," I said through clenched teeth. Steve must have noted my reddening face or balled fists and quickly changed his approach.

"I'm a sales rep for Box Store Company, and I'd like to show you some products we have for small restaurants such as this."

"Oh yeah, sure, we are actually looking for a paper product provider...say that three times fast!" I shot Steve the finger guns, at which he stared back at blankly. Steve and I did not share the same sense of humour, it seemed.

"Well, I'd just be more comfortable speaking with you and your husband about this, so why don't I leave you this catalogue, and we can set up a time to do business that works best for everyone."

"Um okay. Sounds good. I'm Lindsay, by the way." My words were lost as Steve was already shuffling out the door. The meeting left me feeling uncomfortable and wondering what had just happened.

"Hi Steve, this is Lindsay Brown from the Hot Wire Panini. I'm just calling to place an order with you."

"Oh. Hello."

"So, can I place that order, Steve?"

"Ahem, uh, yeah, let me grab my computer." A moment's pause. "Okay, what would you like?"

As I gave Steve our order a week after our initial meeting, I had almost forgotten about the ill-at-ease feeling this man had given me. But just before I hung up, he said, "You know Linds," I was not aware Steve and I were on a name-shortening basis, but I let it slide. "Linds, I'd just feel more comfortable about this order if I could okay it with your husband first."

"Jamie wrote the order down for me to give to you. I have a list in his handwriting in front of me, Steve. He okays it. You can take my word."

"Well..." Steve's blatant refusal to acknowledge me as a responsible human being was beginning to wear on me.

"Goddammit, Steve, just do your mother fucking job, man!" is what I wanted to scream at the person on the other end of the phone, but I was wary of doing so. Wary because we were new business owners in a new city, and in these first delicate years, I believed we should mind our Ps and Qs.

So instead, I said, "Steve. Steve. I've got to say, man, I really appreciate your attentiveness. I really do. But Jamie is so busy right now. You know, with running an entire business by himself. Steve, buddy, I just don't think he's going to have time to approve it, man. Do you think you could just let it go this one time, Steve?"

"Oh well, that's no problem! Why didn't you say so? I'll just come on down and meet Jamie in person. Right now." And that is exactly what Steve did. He came on down.

During Steve's visit to our shop, he explained his absolute hatred for women due to his recent, messy divorce. Somehow the hardships placed on him by this one specific woman transferred to the entirety of the female race being untrustworthy and heinous. He relayed his sad story of marriage and divorce in full detail. All the while glaring maliciously in my general direction as though his ex may well materialize at any moment out of my dastardly vagina.

Steve then went on to plead with hands locked in a prayer-like gesture. "Please, oh please, call me if you need anything. Call me day or night. Call me if there is anything. You know, sometimes people say they are going to call and then they don't. So please, just call . . . I'm very. Very. Serious."

It was uncomfortable.

In the end, we finalized the order merely to get him to leave our store. In the weeks to come, we would try to call Steve several more times to voice our complaints about the shitty products we received from Box Store Company. But to our simultaneous relief and mounting curiosity, we never saw Steve again. Eventually, we would begin to wonder if Steve had ever really existed at all.

Or, possibly, he was just a figment of our imagination, rummaged up from the intense stress and pressure that comes along with opening a sandwich shop.

Thirty-Five

Sometimes I like to wander around the pond in the wealthy part of the city and pretend that I'm rich. I don't know what it's like to be rich, so this makes my musings boundless. My fantasies don't have to include all the drama that I assume comes with wealth. I just get to Scrooge McDuck into my arena-sized room full of gold coins. Glamorous, I know.

As I walk, I notice a lot of other people like me. People whose houses don't back onto a glamorous man-made pond. My kids and I call this place Storm Ponds. We call it this because I misread the information plaque upon first learning of the place. Instead of seeing that it was a storm pond used to store overflow water during the rainy season, I thought the name of the area was literally Storm Ponds. Storm Ponds! It's actually called Chinook Ponds but I think Storm Ponds is better.

The spot is beautiful. There's a wide walking path surrounding the water, cattails sprout along the outer banks, and there's even a tiny inlet island with a gazebo where one might go for a picnic. The houses that encircle the pond and path are mansions.

I am most infatuated with this deep chocolate brown house. It has three separate patios jutting out from the back of it. The one on the ground level has an enormous hot tub equipped with a breathtakingly pretentious built-in towel room. The next deck level is mid-way up the home's exterior off what I assume is the living room. An array of tropical plants are artfully displayed in the floor-to-ceiling windows and the patio has a mind-boggling amount of outdoor furniture upon it. The white wicker sectional couch is hashtag life goals.

The last deck, the most intriguing, is on the top floor. It may be smaller than the rest, and yet I feel it's the most opulent. I assume it must be the master bedroom. Can you imagine having a deck right off your main bedroom? Sounds *amaze*. If this were my outdoor deck off my main bedroom, I'd be out there, buck ass nakey every morning, sun tanning my butthole because that's supposed to be really healthy for a person. After my butthole had an adequate soaking of Vitamin D I'd sip flavoured coffee on my white wicker lounger and write nonsensical stories on an ancient typewriter because that's just the kind of person I'd be if I were rich.

I know how this sounds. Anyone with money will shake their head at my words, saying, "It's not all great, sister, I can tell you that much. Money isn't everything." Because they will be thinking about their shitty relationships and the fact that their thirteen-year-old dog still died from cancer despite the thousands of dollars they spent on vet bills. Those people will swear up and down that money doesn't buy happiness. They'll say they would give up their material assets tomorrow if only it would bring their family closer together. If only it would bring Lassie or Brutus or whatever their dog's name was back to life. Like some freaky-ass dog zombie. And to that, I say, bullshit.

If you've never had to feed your family with the twelve dollars left in your overdraft, then please understand this simply doesn't concern you. Money, if you have it, is nothing but a passing fancy. If you don't have it, money is the driving force for your very existence. One rotten rung on your life ladder and there you go tumbling to the ground, with no savings account to cushion the fall.

Yes, I have a home, my kids are fed, and I can drink the occasional glass of wine when I feel sad. I have luxuries that many don't, and I'm eternally thankful for that, but living without a savings account or backup funds is scary. People look at you differently when they realize you're almost forty years old and still living paycheck to paycheck.

The debt that looms over our heads from a bad business venture haunts us every day. Chipping away at consolidated debt repayment is like panning for gold from a stream gone dry. You're doing it for the idea of "one day," but at the moment, it's all looking pretty damn grim. Money doesn't buy people happiness, but it does an excellent job of purchasing some high-grade security.

The Storm Pond houses are big and beautiful. The lawns are perfectly manicured, and the pond that's mere feet away is filled with Canadian Geese. A jogger nods curtly as she glides past me. She isn't looking at the houses—she must live in this community. You see, that's the tell. That's what lets me know if my fellow walkers are residents of this place or mere interlopers pretending to be someone else for a short while.

No one who lives in this place would gawk at these houses. My peering, my staring into a life-that-will-never-be, confirms my outsider status.

I am startled out of my reverie by the sound of loud honking. Multiple honks. Flapping wings. All swarming in my direction, as if they know I don't belong.

Oh, for the love of poutine, not the Canadian Geese!

This is the downside of Storm Ponds. The geese think they own the place. Even though there is such luxury behind the fences of these homes, the geese are a cruel reminder that no one is all that special if they dare to walk the goose shit littered path. Long grayish-white turds sully the cement and green spaces in the park. The geese feel free to roam as they please, and on more than one occasion, I've had to take a ten-minute detour to avoid the significant goose gangs as they sprawl on sun-heated sidewalks. I've learned it is not wise to skirt the territorial beasts. And although the rich people in Storm Ponds don't care about me gazing in at their homes with wonder, the geese sure fucking do.

This is to say, there have been many goose chases. I finally understand the game Duck, Duck, Goose. Only a goose would get heated enough to give chase when being plunked on the head by a tiny child's hand.

So, there it is, distracted for only a few seconds by the large houses, and now, regrettably, a gander of geese is hurtling toward me. I'm praying to all the gods in all the lands that I can make it back to my 2006 hand-me-down Jeep Cherokee before the geese accost me. My legs pump wildly. My heart is hammering against my ribcage. And yet, they gain.

It's then I remember that the automatic unlock button on my Jeep is busted. I huddle low by the driver's side door, hoping to evade their deadly battle cries. Luckily, the geese are not out for blood, not today, at least.

With a relieved sigh, I manually unlock the door, climb into my jeep, and notice the jogger running at full speed on the path. Her arms flail outrageously as she turns her head to view her attackers. The geese are right behind her. I see she is headed toward a far-off gate leading to a home not much smaller than the one with three balconies. I start my car and honk the horn, hoping to distract our feathered foes for just a little while so she can make her escape successfully. As I'm blaring on the buzzer, it occurs to me that, quite possibly, the only thing that Canadian Geese are good for is their impartial nature when choosing their victims.

I see the woman dash through her gate, not stopping to close it behind her. Before I know it, she is locked up in her own hot tub towel room off her first-floor patio as the geese mill nonchalantly about in her yard. I figure she can take it from there; she's probably got some kind of fancy bottled water to sustain her for a little while, at least.

Thirty-Six

Starting a business is scary, but starting a business while also moving your family to a new city where you know no one? It's insanity, plain and simple. Mine and Jamie's brains were on a one-track course at the time: **create yummo food+sell many panini=make mega dollars!** I don't know why our one-track course sounds like a drunken teenage Neanderthal but that's just what happens when you're feeling desperate I guess. Despite our desperation, I still needed to look after my family while Jamie focused on building the business.

Acquiring a family doctor in our new city was paramount. Doctors are in high demand around these parts. We may have free healthcare but finding yourself a free healthcare professional to see on a regular basis might prove to be a bit trickier of a proposition. You don't just try on a doctor like a hat here in Canada. It's the other way around. You put on a beautiful little monkey dance for them, presenting your various triumphs and failures in the personal health department, and they decide if you're worthy of their doctorage.

I had booked a meeting with a potential family doc in the morning, as I knew I could not afford the appointment to run into the lunch hour. After our meet and greet, Doctor E casually asked when I had last undergone a pap smear.

Immediately clenching up, I advised him, "I, uh, umm, I don't remember?"

I remembered. For some reason, my brain thought that if I avoided his inquiry, this doctor might forget he had asked the question in the first place.

My plan failed. "Well, if you can't even remember, then I am going to book you in for one immediately," Doctor E said.

"Oh. Well, I do have to get to work soon," I tried.

"I insist we get this done. It will only take a few minutes."

"Okay," I said resignedly and then began peeling away my clothes—forgetting all the doctor-patient etiquette I had learned over the past thirty years.

"Oh, please stop doing that," he said. "The examination isn't done in this room. Nurse Catherine will perform the pap smear in the room down the hall."

"I see," I replied.

"Yes. You can leave now."

I had the distinct feeling our relationship had started on an awkward note.

As with all pap smears, the experience was cold and sterile. It left me feeling like I would never quite get used to this womanhood thing. The nurse performing the check-up was kind and knew what she was doing. Nevertheless, when a stranger is shoving foreign equipment into your body, you find yourself thankful you won't have to see them again anytime soon.

Except that's not at all what happened.

I walked into the restaurant to find Jamie with a lineup of customers, which gave way to a mix of emotions. I was excited that our place was catching on with the community. Guilty that I had missed the first part of the rush. And slightly uncomfortable. That was probably due to the metal speculum that had been prodding my cervix a mere fifteen minutes before.

Putting aside all the feelings, I did as any committed customer service person does during a rush: I hopped in front of the cash register and got to work. I was making a coffee and had just turned around to greet my next customer when there, standing before me, was Nurse Catherine.

The very nurse who, only short minutes before, had been staring into the great wonder of my vagina.

"Oh, hello," I said awkwardly. "Fancy seeing you here." I then stress-screamed internally for a while because I'm not the kind of person who does well in a you've-just-seen-my-lady-parts-and-now-I'm-serving-you-food type situation.

"Hey, girl," she said in a casual girlfriend-like tone. "Do you own this place?"

It's like she didn't remember what had just happened. Like she wasn't thinking about my nethers as she ordered her Monte Cristo panini.

"Oh yeah, I do," I replied, unable to grasp the situation unfolding before me. At this point, Jamie was looking at me strangely, his eyebrows raised quizzically. I turned around so my back faced Catherine. As I dished her bowl of soup, I silently mouthed this sentence to my husband:

"That woman just saw my vagina," while rolling my eyes in Catherine's direction.

I should have chosen my words differently. Jamie wasn't aware that, as of recently, this woman and I had a sort of history. Thus, he could not understand why I was hysterically mouthing the word vagina at him.

When she had finished eating, I made my way over to Catherine's table. Despite the deep-down feelings accompanied by the strange combination of a pap smear and a hot-pressed sandwich, I still had to do my job. Which was, at this point, clearing Catherine's table and asking if she enjoyed her meal.

"Oh, wow, I am just so glad we found this place," Catherine said. "It's so close to the clinic! We're going to come here all the time for lunch."

"Yay," I said unenthusiastically.

"You guys keep up the great work," Catherine offered as she and her coworker got up to leave.

Then, as if a small and wretched demon had taken over my brain, I called after her, "You're great at your job too!"

Thirty-Seven

I've been called clumsy. I've also been called downright inelegant. On any given day, I might fall up a flight of stairs or awkwardly say, "How's about some Lindsay lovin'?" to my husband when I'm feeling frisky. Then I'll trip over thin air as I attempt to sexually saunter toward him. I am challenged in the way of high-heel walking, although I try my darndest when invited to fancy parties—which is hardly ever. Those who know me well absentmindedly ready themselves to catch me as I fall while walking down a steep hill or rocky pathway because they are confident I'll eventually end up on my face.

I've always dreamed of demanding a room's attention upon entering. I yearn to be one of those well-spoken women that everyone is naturally drawn to. Despite being in mid-sentence or having a mouthful of mashed potato stuffed into your craw, as soon as they enter a room, your jaw will drop, and you become utterly speechless upon having this person's presence bestowed upon you.

Well, actually, I do request the attention of a room upon entrance. This is not due to my classic elegance. But rather, my rambling incompetence when taking part in any social situation ever. I make myself known by tripping over a carpet or gagging randomly on the spit accumulating in my mouth. Being human is so weird sometimes.

This is all to say, it's incredible I didn't kill anyone while we owned our sandwich shop. Handling dangerous kitchen equipment was something I should have never overseen. I am reminded of the time I nearly scalded myself and a nearby patron while working a lunch rush at the shop.

I was carrying a tray of two soups and a glass of water to a customer on the opposite side of the restaurant. Our restaurant was not enormous. Two-seater tables lined the walls, and extended window seating ran the length of three bay windows facing the street.

I turned the corner that led from behind the service counter, out toward the tables, and somehow found the one small puddle of water resting solitary on the floor. From there, I slid. Both feet did a drunken jig, attempting to right themselves, while a tidal wave of jalapeno popper soup swamped me in great globs of spicy degradation.

In my panic, I assumed that the man who was reaching out to me was attempting to push me further into this mortifying situation. Why a customer would do such a thing is beyond me, but I suppose that my mistrust of human beings in general goes much deeper than I had initially thought. So instead of allowing this gentleman to assist me, I contorted my body away from him. Resulting in me nearly splashing soup all over a woman in a very expensive pantsuit. She was sitting with her son, just trying to have a nice lunch.

After stabilizing myself, I asked if I had gotten her with the soup. The woman was kind and said no. However, I did see her wipe away some rouge liquid off her pant leg out of the corner of my eye as I turned to leave.

"Oh no!" I wailed when seeing I had, in fact, soiled her fancy pantsuit. "I did get you with the soup! And your suit looks so expensive. Can I pay for your dry cleaning? Here, let me try to wipe it off for you!" As I brought the disgusting kitchen towel I was holding closer to her otherwise pristine pantsuit she recoiled in horror.

"No, no, it's fine, truly. Don't worry." I wasn't convinced, but the look Jamie gave me said I should leave well enough alone. I noted a large glob dripping down the woman's open-toed high heel, making me think of the water shoes.

When we were twelve, Janelle and I spent our summer in the water. Feral and free, we boasted sunburned skin and wild, knotted hair. Janelle had recently been given a beautiful new pair of water shoes. They were made of an airy, lightweight material. This was to avoid the disgusting lake bottom that always resulted in sore feet due to rock stabbings and leech attacks.

I didn't want to look like an idiot and admit that I didn't have these fancy water shoes, so instead, I walked right into the lake with my thick-soled gym shoes, double-knotted laces, and all. I'm not sure what I was trying to accomplish by doing such a thing, Janelle was a smart kid; she knew they weren't water shoes. Maybe I was simply trying to fool myself? Regardless, swimming was difficult that day. The added weight of the wet track shoes was not helping my plight. I had affixed a five-pound burden to each foot due to the excess liquid the shoes sucked up.

With each failed watersault (summersault in the water) and top-heavy handstand that resulted in my legs crashing seaward in a colossal wave of disappointment, I felt like a water-shoeless loser.

I made a squishy squashing sound with each heavy step on the sidewalk. This was all my parent's fault. Why would they have forsaken me like this and not bought me the water shoes I so clearly needed? Trudging back to Janelle's house, large shoe-shaped water spots staining the sidewalk, I was miserable. Then it happened. I somehow rolled my ankle on the curb of the sidewalk, and I went down hard. I crashed onto the cement while tiny droplets of shoe water came spitting up over me. The humiliation was long and lasting. What made it worse was the gales of laughter coming from Janelle as she reached her hand down to help me up.

I told her to shut up and shoved her hand away. It wasn't so bad when I believed it was just her who had witnessed my fall. Then I realized a large group of people was standing in a nearby yard. They watched with concern as I attempted to heave myself up, my sopping wet shoes oppressing my ability to move stealthily.

"Are you okay?" a man yelled from his porch.

I looked in the direction of the voice. A gaggle of looky-loos stood watching the grand entrance I made simply walking in front of their homes. I grabbed Janelle by the hand and told her to just keep walking. Pay no attention to the group of concerned adults to the left of us. I hobbled the rest of the way home with soggy shoes, both knees packed with gravel debris and blood trickling down my leg.

"I'm fine," I told Janelle's mom, Terry, as we got to the house. "I just need a Band-Aid." Because Terry is a woman who does not suffer fools, she left me to it and didn't ask many questions. For this, I was thankful.

The woman's shoes in the restaurant looked well worn but expensive, and I couldn't help but think, much like in my situation years ago, something as simple as a pair of good water shoes would have made all the difference.

Thirty-Eight

"The great thing about owning a sandwich shop is that you get to daydream while working and not catch shit for it." - LRB

I stood at a cluttered prep table, slicing a large log of pepperoni into thin strips for the day's sandwiches. As I neared the end of the tube, I stopped and stared bewilderingly at the cusp of that cured meat conduit. On the pork cylinder's tip, where the thin casing ends, there appeared to be a sphincter. A meat sphincter.

If you haven't spent a lot of time around meat pistons, this might be a difficult thing to envision. Unfortunately, googling "Pictures of Meat Sphincters" goes against my better judgment. Either way, something like a butthole had formed at the end of the tube due to the puckering from the casing over the cylinder's stump.

Why did my brain immediately think of a butthole?
I wondered if I was the first person to make this assessment?
Should I ask Jamie, who was slicing bread a few feet away?
I needed to let him know about this fantastic discovery.

"*Let me hit you with a fact, my friend,*" I'd confidently say. He would have looked at me quizzically, which would give me the chance to go into detail about my find. Jamie would shake his head and chuckle. He wouldn't see the beauty in the thing: a butthole in a ginormous meat tube. And then I'd get mad that he thought I was being funny when really, I was thinking I was onto something here.

Ten minutes later, we'd be arguing about meat assholes, and I'd say something like, "You're the meathead, asshole!" And as stupid as it sounds, it would hurt his feelings, and then we wouldn't talk for a while, and it would be awkward when one of us finally broke down and had to apologize over our stupid fight about meat assholes.

Instead of informing my better half of the discovery, I stayed quiet and continued slicing. Oh puckered brown-eye of the meat stick, I shall celebrate you reverently, but also, silently.

Five years ago, Jamie and I were drinking beer on our front stoop with our new neighbour, Tim. We were joking about the colour of our houses. On our street were sparkling white and cream-coloured homes; cool, sleek-looking houses of greys and blacks; and then two light pink atrocities. Not even salmon, but pastel rose-coloured abominations. Come to think of it, our matching house colours were probably why Jamie and I immediately bonded with Tim. It's true what they say, find another person who lives in a pink house, and you'll be friends forever.

"But, you sort of have to admit, our houses are the colour of a cat's asshole," Tim said as he took another swig of his Kokanee. "Sphincter Pink," he proclaimed as if declaring the colour an official title. His voice was authoritative and confident, which immediately led us to believe that Sphincter Pink was precisely what the home builders had in mind. I don't know about Jamie, but at that moment, I had buttholes on the brain. A hodgepodge of rectal images began to float through my mind. As though the clouds had parted and I saw King Mufasa himself in all his liony glory, I knew Tim was onto something transcendent.

"My God, it is Sphincter Pink!" Jamie agreed, awestruck by Tim's astuteness. To the left of us, our very conservative neighbours slammed their kitchen window shut in the passive-aggressive manner to which we had become accustomed.

"Sphincter Pink," I mused quietly, reflecting upon the phonetic nature of the phrase. There sat three twenty-somethings, purring over the word "sphincter" while gazing attentively at the house beyond a stoop. In the years to follow, long after we had moved out of our sphincter pink home, Jamie and I would still find ourselves rummaging up this memory. It became a sort of lore in our fading recollections.

"Remember when we got drunk with Tim and were yelling the phrase Sphincter Pink throughout the neighbourhood?"

"Those were the glory days, my friend."

I looked down at my meat sphincter nestled on a prep table in a little sandwich shop and thought about creating new lore, new memories. I noticed Jamie watching me gaze at the wrinkled end of this pepperoni log, and he smiled kindly.

"Whatcha thinking about, Lin?" he asked cautiously, as though speaking to a discombobulated raccoon.

I would tell him. I would loudly exclaim my ideas about meat sphincters and pepperoni butts. However, I realized that sometimes these things must remain in the sanctity of one's own grotesque mind. That small, private crook of our imagination where Batman is an erotic pole dancer who purrs in his sultry, deep-set Batman voice, "Lindsay Rae Brown is the funniest woman I have ever known. And beautiful too. She's the whole package." That crevice of the brain where you fully expect to win the lottery one day despite having never actually purchased a lottery ticket. Finally, you could buy that dancing pole and Batman costume you've had your eye on.

It is that secret place where you lock away the desires you cannot voice to the world. The area where you hide your deepest darkest worries. The obsessive wondering over whether our dreams will ever become a reality. That small corner of fear telling us we aren't smart enough. Funny enough. Good enough to get what we so desperately feel might essentially complete us. This is where I would store the memory of my pepperoni sphincter.

As for the meatstick itself? Countless customers enjoyed that pork sausage on their paninis that day. And each time I saw them smile after taking a bite, I silently saluted my pepperoni butthole.

Thirty-Nine

During our three-year run, we only had to ban one person from the restaurant. This seems pretty good, considering I come from a town where business owners are continuously banning drunkards and teen hooligans from their various stores and eateries.

Greg wasn't a terrible person when we first met him. He was a large round man who had a severe face and said what was on his mind. I met Greg in the middle of a busy lunch rush. I was sweating and getting a little angsty at the prospect of serving another fifty people before the day ended when a man in an absurdly baggy shirt and shorts came and stood beside me at the register.

"Oh. Hello," I said, not understanding why this person was so close to me.

"You must be Mrs. Brown. Good work, James," he shouted to my husband, who was making sandwiches on the other side of the line. And because I am pretty much the whitest lady ever, the blush that filled my cheeks was deep and seemingly everlasting.

"You're especially cute when you blush like that," Greg laughed. He then threw a twenty at me and ordered a smoked beef panini. Later Jamie explained that Greg had come in the previous night after I had left. Greg was smitten with our large sandwiches and us, apparently, because he began making daily visits to our little sandwich shop.

Greg became a regular fixture over the following months. He would come in, fire inappropriate comments toward me, laugh it off and order lunch.

For most of my life, I have flown my feminist flag loud and proud. I've stood on a chair and yelled, "I am a feminist!" as Caitlin Moran suggested in *How to be a Woman*. I've read *The Female Eunuch* by Germaine Greer, had mixed thoughts about it, and began to form my own ideas about feminism and equality by gathering up as much information as I can and sorting that shit for myself. Ultimately, I just try to stand tall beside my fellow gals.

Now I had this misogynistic dude hanging around the shop, and although he was funny and was spending a good fortune on our food, I had a shitty feeling about him. He was brash. He was in my face. Greg went out of his way to make others feel small.

I don't know about your city, but here in Lethbridge, Pride month is awesome. There are so many opportunities to learn about 2SLGBTQ+ people and issues, and everything is rainbow clad. We celebrated by baking rainbow baked goods for the month and would donate the proceeds from those goodies to our city's Pride organization. We also were pretty vocal on our social media channels that there would be no tolerance for hate speech in our establishment.

Of course, there are always the nonentities who scream the loudest when they have nothing of value to say. We'd hear a lot of things like, "I don't care what they do in the privacy of their own home, but why do they need a parade for it? Where's my straight pride parade?" As if being gay, transgender or queer was some sort of a private shame one should keep to themselves. The thing about privilege is that you can smell it dripping off of accusatory statements like this one.

As business owners, we have a choice to get involved in societal issues like this or stay out of them altogether. From a business standpoint, I suppose the right thing to do is stay out of it. You know, so as not to lose any potential customers. But really, where's the fun in that?

Once again, we were busy at the shop. The line was growing, and each person who walked in the door was just a little dollar sign in my brain. Then I saw Greg.

"Hey, did you hear about those stupid crosswalks getting vandalized?" He was talking about the rainbow crosswalks that the Pride committee had painted a few days before.

"Yeah, what kind of an idiot would do that?" I said, trying to avoid his opinion, although I knew in my heart it was coming.

"Well, I wasn't the one who tarred it. Would have if I had the tar, though. I did a few burnouts on the fucking things."

And that's when my world stopped. The chatter of the customers quieted to a dull hum. Jamie was telling me to drop it. But his words were deep in the background, they were the furthest thing from my mind. My hands balled into fists, and I growled, "Get the hell out of my restaurant."

"Excuse me?" said Greg.

"Get out, man. We don't serve bigots here. Get. The. Fuck. Out." Okay, okay, it wasn't very professional to use the fuck word in front of customers, but at that moment, I didn't care.

"You going to let her do that, man?" Greg yelled to Jamie as if Jamie were going to react differently.

"She's the boss."

I plopped Greg's food on the counter in front of him and told him he wasn't welcome back. And I never saw Greg again.

Forty

Dear Lady with The Enchanting Blue Eye Shadow,

    I'm sorry. I am sorry that I was not able to procure your legal name and now must address you by specific details of your stereotypical accoutrements. More so, I am sorry that I tried to pull the wool over your eyes. It is true. I set out to build a rip-off joint. My master plan was to conceal the thing as a sandwich shop specializing in house-made bread and pastries. Then you came along with your bob-cut and long red fingernails and caught me red-handed.

    I can see why you were perturbed. It was scandalous that my handcrafted pastry tarts were slightly more expensive than the ones sitting in a display case for the last three days at the gas station down the road. Honestly, I'm surprised you were the first to be peeved by such an underhanded business move.

    The thing is, I couldn't in good conscience leave our meet and greet hanging as it did: you running out of the store while screaming obscenities at me and shaking your fist. It just doesn't feel right. So here and now, I want to lay it on the line for you and reveal my evil plan.

    A few years back, I set out to open a small business called the Hot Wire Panini in order to rob people blind.

    It was the perfect plan. It struck me that if I made the pastry and bread by hand and from scratch, I might further the illusion of an authentic small business.

Do not misunderstand me, though; ripping people off was always the end goal. I sacrificed. Feeding the community with real, unprocessed foods disgusted me. I was, after all, evil to the bone. When small children would approach me exclaiming in their lispy voices, "I love your thandwiches and cookies," I'd nearly puke myself. Eventually, as my erroneous business grew in popularity, I was forced to contribute to charitable events in the community. Gross. But what else could I do? I was backed into a corner and had to keep up the façade. So I held a few bake sales where the profits went to organizations like the local food bank or the hottest new disease campaign. I chalked it up to the life of a con man and begrudgingly carried on with the work.

Of course, one gets to know their patrons after running a business for a while. Some of these dupes regrettably grew on me. Consequently, I ended up catering a few of their weddings at cost as favours to the bride and groom. But it was all in the name of a higher cause. The ripping-off-my-community cause.

Now it's all over. My inglorious plans of cheating people via a mom-and-pop shop have been foiled. I can't help but wonder how you caught on to my woeful ways. I really believed I had hatched the perfect scheme.

I'll never forget the day it all ended. There you were, screaming at me, little pellets of spittle flinging from your mouth and directly onto my face. You graciously showed me the error of my ways.

"What are you trying to run here?" you demanded incredulously as you stared down at the price of the freshly baked tart. "Some kind of rip-off joint?"

I tried to talk my way out of it. Stupid me! You were too slick to believe my excuse of having to "cover my costs and labour" bullshit. I can't deny your brilliance, that's for sure. You sure know a rip-off joint when you see one. Of course, I was bound to get caught. Local businesses are notorious for their criminal undertakings. Why didn't I think bigger? Why didn't I frame myself as one of those multi-billion-dollar chain gangs that slide glutinous pucks out of Cryovaced baggies and claim it is healthier than freshly baked bread? The answer was right in front of me this entire time.

•

So here we are: me, the ruthless small business con artist, apologizing to you, the woman who clearly knows a lot more about small business than the Red Seal chef who's worked in the industry for twenty years and owns said business. I hope this apology is enough to put your wrestling mind at ease. For it is the blue-lidded, bob-cut ladies of the world who will set right the mayhem engendered by small business owners across the country.

I want to thank you, Lady with The Enchanting Blue Eye Shadow, for opening my eyes. I've shut down my dastardly business and am pursuing the more noble career of ghostwriting erotic fan fiction for a large corporation that profits from my work with no credit to me. The change of pace humbles me.

I hope you have not had any more encounters with "swindlers and cheats" recently, and I wish you well in all your future endeavours.

Yours eternally,
A Humbled Small Business Owner

Forty-One

December 2018

    Globules of tears ran down my mascara-lined face. I was hyperventilating. I could not breathe. Jamie sat opposite, with tears rolling down his cheeks, bloodshot eyes, and that familiar furrow to his brow. Between us was a kitchen table full of debt. The lines of credit, the overdue bills, and the overdraft notices we had accumulated since starting our business.

    "We can't keep going like this," he said.

    "We can't stop," I said. "We can't just quit."

    "It's not working. The business plan isn't working. We don't have enough people coming in. We will have to go bankrupt by year-end if this keeps up." He swept his hand over the table as if he was showing off a horde of precious goods.

    "But the business is good. People love it." I pleaded. There was something in my voice that I hated. Something pensive and fussy that I had never heard before. Desperation.

    If we shut down our little sandwich shop that we had poured so much into, what would I have? What would make me unique? What a pathetic exposé of Lindsay Rae Brown. The girl who craved the limelight.

    "What will I do after it's gone?" I asked with surprising clarity.

    The kids were growing fast and would soon be working on their own life projects. Although their dad and I would always be there for them first and foremost, I believe as parents we must continue to carve out our own hopes and desires during the child-rearing years. You know, so not to become one of those, live-vicariously-through-your-kid type people. If we did not have a business to coddle, where would that leave me?

Jamie took me in his arms and kissed my forehead in the same way he had always done. The way he did when we first stood in his mother's basement, young, stoned, and unaffected by the ways of this harsh world, and he told me he loved me for the first time.

"You'll write," he whispered in my ear. We held each other in our kitchen, unease leaking out of our brains and onto a dirty floor.

Small business is complicated in the best of times. Ideally, new owners have a secondary income to live off while building their business up. Allowing all monies that come in to stay there to nurture growth and development within the company.

We moved to our current city to start a sandwich shop. And to all intents and purposes, it was a success. Even the books said so. After the first full year, we had turned a small profit. Any money we made went directly back into the business. We survived off our credit cards and the leftover food from the restaurant. We did this for three years. We did what any great entrepreneur tells a new business owner not to do. We made the thing our baby. We sacrificed for it. We went without in order to feed the business.

In the end, the business sank us. Although the company looked okay (not great, but okay) on paper, if anyone were to take a look into our personal finances, they would likely pull a Wile E. Coyote and run for the hills through a brick wall. We had been supplementing our meagre income with credit for three years, and finally, the credit had run out.

Six months after our kitchen table realization, I was clearing out the restaurant's bay. Rather than sell the business, we dissolved it. What a morbid turn of phrase. We murdered our dreams and liquefied them in a tub of acid. It was an accurate description of how dissolving a business feels.

Emotions whipped through the air on invisible jet streams, waiting to strike at any given moment. I might be scrubbing a particularly tough stain off the floor where the deep freeze once sat, wondering what's in store for me next, when the desperation hit. It slid in through my ear and burrowed into my consciousness. There it pecked away, unearthing the failure, the colossal botch this endeavour had become. I was never less confident than the day I handed over the keys to an empty bay, which once housed our budding little business.

Forty-Two

When one finds themselves on a hot and busy line in the throes of a lunch rush, there is no time for logic. Instead, we revert to a prehistoric and, quite frankly, animalistic tendency. We make decisions based solely on survival.

- What will get the fastest results?

- Will this jeopardize the food?

- How do I slap a smile on my face while this know-it-all customer tells me for the tenth time that I should really think about hiring staff because "it's pretty busy in here"?

It always happens the same way. All is quiet until the stampede approaches. Noon draws nearer and with it comes the feeding hour. As though a silent bell reverberates in the brains of the average working Joe, the people move inward to the sandwich shop. The smells of crisping bacon and baking bread bring a dribble of saliva to their lips. Moaning, they scour the menu. They are ravenous in their contemplations and ready to devour the fare placed in front of them.

As you watch them pile in the door, mouths watering, eyes hungry for the food waiting so close yet so far away behind the sneeze guard, you have the lingering notion that it all feels a bit apocalyptic. Like, how the hell are you, one person, supposed to feed all these human beings? Fear not, dear server; the trick is not in the serving itself but instead in how you look at the horde of hangry people as a whole.

Chanting the soundless mantra, "It cannot last forever," you begin.

Smile, greet, take the order, make the food, repeat. You do this as mindlessly as possible. Interruptions cause issues. Dress the bread, tower the meat, sprinkle the cheese, press the sandwich. This is now your life until the lineup is no more.

Usually, you can get through the rush with little to no mishaps. Usually.

It was the day before we closed the shop permanently. We had made the official Facebook announcement to our patrons, explaining that running the business was becoming increasingly difficult for just me. Jamie had already taken the position at the railroad as a train conductor in order to save us from financial ruin. It was simply not financially viable to keep the Hot Wire open. Especially since we did not see any potential buyers on the horizon.

As with all official announcements on social media, a plethora of "suggestions" poured in from people who had the answer to the question we were not asking.

"Well, why don't you just hire staff?" a well-intentioned customer wrote. Oh. My. God. Why the hell didn't I think of hiring staff? Well, geez, Louise, we could have avoided losing our business and having to do the hardest thing of our lives by just hiring a few staff members. Shucks, I'm so mad I didn't think of that.

I don't want to be one of those business owners, but I will lay the cold hard facts on you. A minimum wage worker costs fifteen dollars an hour here in Alberta (which we were happy to pay, don't get me wrong). However, the living wage in our city should be $20.50. Meaning to live comfortably, you must make $20.50/hour. Unfortunately, we could not afford to pay $20.50. Hell, we weren't bringing home $20.50.

Finding someone who was multitasked in the ways of running a till, able to speak and make eye contact with customers—this was actually a very rare trait to come across—was difficult enough. To find someone who could handle their own during a lunch rush and take it upon themselves to clean as well, was a tall ask for a minimum wage paying job. Not to mention the looming threat that we were trying to sell the business. Prospective employees weren't into it, and I don't blame them.

Another helpful chap wrote on our very public page that anyone looking for equipment should message us because, and I quote, "They are probably going broke and will need the money." Look, friend, we were broke long before we decided to sell this place. Thank you very much!

So, it was the day before we closed, and I was managing the lunch rush solo. It's funny how it all buffed out; for months, we had just been scraping by because, who knows, we were old news or whatever, but as soon as we announced our farewell, everyone told us how much we were loved and appreciated in the community.

I don't want to be bitter. I know it gives me worry lines. But come on, people. Why does the lady from the print shop down the road feel the need to tell me how angry she is that we're closing because we made the best damn sandwich she'd ever tasted? She said this as a dollop of mayo rested lazily on the ridge of her chin. I smiled and nodded. Commiserating with her woes, I decided not to tell her about the mayo, a small but seemingly fitting way to part our short friendship.

I want to tell all these people, in the short, clipped voice of an overworked, underpaid, highly irritated elementary school teacher, that if they support small businesses, then this does not happen. They do not close their doors. They continue to grow and flourish and become the large chain stores that they all hated so desperately in the first place. It's like this vicious circle of consumerism that we have all grown to accept.

As I switched on the OPEN sign and unlocked the doors, I saw that I was already faced with a sidewalk full of anticipatory panini people. "Oh, for the love of all things glutinous and cheesy," I whispered as the horror of what was about to befall me came entirely into view.

And it began. A wave of humans rushed the door.

By 11:30 a.m. I realized I was running out of cheese.

By 11:45 a.m. a customer who happened to be a chef hopped on line to assist me in getting through the lineup. He could not stand idly by while I drowned in my own failure as a short-order cook.

By noon I was on the verge of telling every single person in the place to fuck right off and go to Subway down the street.

By 12:10 p.m. I had a little comeback and thought I might just be getting a hold of this thing.

By 12:30 p.m. I was entirely out of bread, meats, and cheeses. I had to tell the twenty-five people who were still in line waiting that I couldn't take any more orders because, apparently, I was a shit restaurateur and did not understand the importance of food preparation before a busy lunch hour.

It was a dark day in the food industry. A dark, dark day. But, like all rushes, I got through it to tell the tale. I guess that goes to show why we ended up having to shut down the restaurant when my husband found a job on the railroad. I, a lowly writer of internet things, was not cut out for the restaurant biz.

Forty-Three

Jamie found a job on the railroad. Cooking is his passion, but in the world of Southern Alberta, cooking was not a financially realistic way to raise a family. A grim verdict. It was another reason the guilt in those first few months splashed over me like droplets of tub acid. The priority is money. There, I said it. The debt hung not over us but beneath us, dragging my husband and me down into the pit of despair. You remember the pit of despair from *The Princess Bride*? In this scenario, our mounting stress was the albino, stripping years off our lives.

When we told Lars and Sophie we were closing the shop, they jumped for joy. Literally. Jamie and I had sat them down on Lars' bed and told them gently that the shop wasn't working, so we'd have to shut it down. The closest thing we received to sadness was Lars tentatively asking if we'd have to move away, because he did not want to leave his friends. We told them no, we were not moving, and our ten and eight-year-olds then proceeded to get feet-side on Lars' bed and do happy dances. Never would they have to sit through a busy lunch rush in the cramped and sort-of-smelly office of the shop again. No longer would we miss school functions or have to decline volunteering obligations because of our responsibilities to the shop. Finally, they could try Subway Sandwiches because this behemoth corporation would no longer be considered our arch enemy. These kids were ecstatic.

I keep this memory wound tight in my mind. I will never let it go. It guards me against moments of self-doubt when wondering if we did the right thing in closing our business. When the what if's start to consume me.

- What if we had fought just a little harder?

- What if we had pursued financial counsel instead of throwing in the towel?

- What if we had dug deeper to find a way out of the hole?

I think of their happy dance, and that helps me move my family forward.

Then it was summer. We had closed the business accounts and wrapped up what we could before our accounting year-end. The summer was ours. It had been years since I had spent the summer with my children. Usually, due to responsibilities to the business, I'd ship them off to our extended family to spend their summer in Sylvan Lake.

I'm not going to lie, it was strange. What would I do? How could I fill the day without working a ten-hour shift? There I was with these two young individuals who were teeming with the exhilaration, and I was at a loss.

So, I asked them, "Do you guys want to go swimming or something?"

I'd like to tell you that we had one specific pool or lake we frequented. Our summer spent at this place, soaking up the sun and living a water-baby life—but that's not exactly true. The truth is more like this: we scoured the city; we tried out pools the way high school seniors try on extravagant fashions for prom. On days when Jamie was off work, we'd hop in the car and journey to new towns to find new pools. We gobbled up swim facilities without remorse. And once we were in the water, having found the lake or pool or swimmin' hole for that day, the feeling that we might drown would float away.

Our first swimming excursion opened my eyes to what I had been missing in my children's lives. As we left the changing room, the kids moved toward the pool's deep end. My heartbeat faltered, and I was just about to holler, *"Wait, what are you doing? You guys can't jump in there!"* when they *did* jump in there. They cannon-balled off the edge and into the water, where not even their tippy-toes could touch the bottom.

The lifeguard must have noted the stricken look on my face as she readied herself to save a couple of idiot kids who couldn't tell the deep end from the shallows. But lo and behold, they popped back up and quickly stroked to the side of the pool. They could swim? When the hell did that happen?

While in the water, our carefreeness kept us afloat. Well, it was buoyancy which kept us afloat, but let's call it carefreeness. The verb 'swim' changed into something more like a proper noun, a self-standing entity that slowly began to restore this broken family unit. *Swim* taught us to trust as we made our way into the murkiness of a dugout lake. The four of us held hands as we explored the unknown water, the sun darkening our exposed shoulders. Together we laughed and gasped when tadpoles tickled our toes. Then, Sophie, always Sophie, would dive in. Her hair stretched over her back as she cut through the frigid water.

Swim gave us the joy we so desperately needed that summer. After defeat, it was our reawakening. Jamie and I could have been mulling over our life, over mistakes made and worries yet to come only hours before, but when we jumped into the water and watched these babes swim and play and laugh in a way that told us we are doing okay, everything else drifted away. Like waxed paper sailboats on a river current, we were, for a few hours, allowed to live in the moment.

The summer of 2019 was strange and beautiful and healing. Jamie and I would lay in bed with tears running down our cheeks, musing over a dream that ended too soon. But, we'd laugh too. We made quiet, lazy love on warm afternoons, and he'd kiss my forehead, and we'd talk about someday.

With Jamie's new trade came an entirely new lifestyle for our family. We took the summer to learn how to live on a railroader's schedule. While Jamie was on-call and waiting for the phone to ring, we swam. Swim helped us navigate all kinds of new waters.

The leaves turned overnight, immediate and jarring. The ash tree shading our living room window revealed a lonely yellow leaf amidst a sea of green. Soon we would be raking together colossal piles of desiccated leaves to take hackneyed photographs, stored away in a computer file called "Fall 2019." Soon we'd be making snowmen who'd go by Frank and Mrs. Shovelton. In no time, we'd be opening Christmas presents and sledding, our mugs of hot chocolate perched at the top of icy hills, promising to keep us warm.

Soon the Hot Wire, which once gave us so much happiness and so much strife, would be behind us. A memory that we could look back on and smile.

"Remember when we owned that little sandwich shop," Jamie will say to me as I read my favourite Margaret Atwood story, and he catches up on current events. We will laugh and wonder what we were thinking but also be thankful we had the guts to take a chance.

This thought will lead to another, and I will say, "But remember the swimming? Remember how much we swam with the kids that following summer?" Enough to jar that single season out of the depths of memory and into present days. Sufficiently dredging up our old pal, Swim.

My husband will kiss me on the forehead, as he always has, and tell me he does remember. He will say, "That was a good summer." And I'll agree.

The worries and the stress of that period of our lives will have long been forgotten. Carried away and scattered by the waves of that once upon summer of Swim.

Forty-Four

I think back through this strange life and can cherry-pick the people who have changed my life in some small and inextricable ways. Sheri, my first real boss, allowed me to live with her and her family on multiple occasions when I felt I had nowhere else to go. Janet, my friend Ashley's mom, also took me in during my late teenage years and taught me about magic and books and the unrelenting idea that everything does happen for a reason. Grandma Jean who showed me how to hone my sense of humour and get a laugh out of anyone.

Nearly a year ago, I needed a friend, and Susie was all like, "Hey, I'm right here, on the other side of this giant ironing press." It's rare to meet someone and understand immediately that you are now connected to them. Usually, that shit takes time. It takes months of chatting and ranting about mutual frustrations to grow a strong bond. I knew Susie and I were destined to be friends after our first shift together.

I tend to be shy around new people and try to hide all my weirdness under my psoriasis-riddled skin. I will myself to go mute because I know if I allow the words to start flowing out of my mouth, some strange non sequitur will eventually fall out like, "Oh, that reminds me of the time my dog sexually assaulted an old man in the park," That story usually results in friends-off.

That never happened with Susie. Don't get me wrong, I've said plenty of weird stuff, but she just takes it in stride. I've never felt that familiar sting of "less-than" when hanging out with Susie. She is a master at making people feel at ease in her presence; at least, that's how she makes me feel. It's a valuable trait to possess, and I appreciate that about her every day.

There is an unspoken rule between us that we will automatically match the rage level the other is clocking on their rage-O-meter so we can feel good about our laundry room vent sessions. Sometimes we talk about politics and world issues, and because Susie is very up to date on her news, I often get a little panicky after she tells me about all the terrible things happening in the world. I, alternatively, need to catch up on my news. I avoid the news. Some might call me an ill-informed baboon. Correction: some *have* called me an ill-informed baboon. Maybe a valid point. Susie has never called me such a thing; she fills me in on what I should probably know as a thirty-seven-year-old woman. Sometimes we talk shit about people. We only do this when it's early in the morning, and we are the only ones in the building because we're respectful like that.

And sometimes, well, one time, we talked about Caterpillar Boy.

Me: Ugh, speaking of movies that should have never been made, have you ever watched The Human Centipede?

Susie: No, never heard of it. What's it about?

Me: HAHA! Hold onto your hat, my friend, because shit's about to get real up in here.

Susie: ...

Me: It's about a mad scientist who kidnaps three random people and then sews them into a singular line attaching the front guy's asshole to the middle guy's mouth and that guy's asshole to that last guy's mouth. He then force-feeds the front guy dog food, and the other two poor saps, well, you get the picture. The two are, unfortunately, forced-fed—via the butthole.

Susie: Excuse me?

Me: Yep.

Susie: That is absolutely horrifying. Is it on Netflix?

Me: Probably.

One Week Later

Susie: Oh hey, I tried to find that movie on Netflix, but I couldn't find it.

Me: Oh?

Susie: Yeah, as soon as I started typing Caterpillar Boy...

Me: Wait. What movie are you talking about?

Susie: You know that messed up movie about the crazy scientist.

Me: *laughing hysterically now* You searched Caterpillar Boy?

Susie: Yeah, isn't that what it's called?

Even after correcting her several hundred times, Susie still calls the movie Caterpillar Boy. I genuinely believe it would have been a better film if it had been called Caterpillar Boy. Could you imagine the devastation that would ensue when tucking into a cute-sounding movie like Caterpillar Boy and coming away with The Human Centipede? Utter revulsion.

Moments like this make me believe in soulmates. Not only the romantic kind but also the friendship kind. When a person you see regularly can cause such uninhibited joy on a day-to-day basis, how can you not believe there are people out there who are meant to be in your life?

Forty-Five

"Oooh," I squealed to Jamie as I rolled over in bed. "Today's the day!"

Jamie was half asleep but groggily draped an arm over me and whispered, "You'll do great, Lind-Bae."

It was a warm spring morning, and I was determined that today would be the day I'd finally become an adult. Of course, being thirty-four at the time, I technically was an adult woman. But considering my previous track record of dealing with adulty things, the odds of being seen as a grown-up weren't in my favour. I was to attend a business meeting that morning, and my excitement was brimming. I had never really been to a business meeting because I am not a very professional person. Maybe the times Jamie and I fooled around in the back storeroom of the shop were considered meetings of a sort, but I had a sneaking suspicion that this would be different.

A few weeks prior, an old acquaintance had found me on Facebook, telling me he loved my social media work lately. Between the self-promotion of my writing and various content work I had done for a local restaurant, he claimed he loved the quirky humour I presented in the marketing world. Mark was building a start-up that had to do with uplifting local businesses and wanted me to head the social media department. Of course, the entire team would consist of him and me, but that didn't dissuade me. I was on board immediately.

I was determined that none of the previous "lindsayisms" that had gotten me into trouble in the past sneak out during our meeting. Today I was wearing my big girl panties, and they were one hundred percent cotton blend. My hair was styled in an important updo, and my paperwork was all filed into a fancy little briefcase dealy at my side. *So expert. Such wow.*

I was sporting a mask, though they hadn't been made mandatory in Alberta yet. So, upon entering the board room where I would be adulting like mad, my business partner invited me to take off my mask. If only I had refused his invitation. If only I had kept it on, therefore avoiding the face touching and gasping under my breath. For you see, it was only about ten minutes into the meeting when I felt something devastating upon my chin.

A long wire thing was jutting out from my skin. I casually prodded around on my face to find what felt like a two-inch long pubic hair growing from my chin.

I don't know why I was so concerned about the hair. Usually, I'm not an exceedingly vain person and can shrug off the awkwardness that comes with being a maturing human being. But the idea of being a professional adult was at the forefront of my mind that day. And now, I figured, all that was going to be threatened by this blasted chin hair.

I considered fessing up about my solitary beard strand to Mark. I could say something like, "Sorry, Mark, I just have to cut you off for a second." He'd probably look at me quizzically, forcing me to push forward. "Do you see this hair I just found on my chin?"

Mark would squint and look closely at my face. But knowing me, I wouldn't leave it at that. While I sat in a boardroom, having an adult business meeting with a fellow I didn't know all that well, I imagined a scenario where I laid it all on the line. Plain as the hair on my chin.

The chin hair reminded me of the time I had a hair growing directly out of my nipple. I had been giving myself a breast exam while showering because I'm very proactive like that, when what to my wondering eyes did appear? A long stiff greying hair sticking straight out of the dead center of my areola.

What the hell was this? Not only the indignity of nipple hair, but greying nipple hair?

I revealed my incredible find to Janelle, looking for some sympathy. I should have known better. She immediately nicknamed me Long John Silver and, regrettably, the name stuck. As did the hair. Never again have I complained about plucking my brows, now that I know the horror of ritualistic nipple plucking.

Poor Mark. There he sat, rambling on about the Facebook badge rewards program while I took in none of it. I was too preoccupied with the memory of my greying nipple hair, twirling my single chin pube in my fingers and wondering if I should bring it up before things got awkward.

I knew that opening my big mouth would only cause more trouble so I willed myself to stay silent on the chin/nipple hair topic.

I left the meeting that day having gleaned two vital pieces of information. One: my job included selling our online product to small business owners in the city. And two: I'd have to invest in some better tweezers.

A week later, I waited by my phone for a call from Mark. There is something about phone calls that make the very depths of my soul quake with fear. If I know that I have a call coming in, I will reschedule all other duties in my life. The kids will have to walk themselves to school. That essay I've been planning to edit can wait until after the call is over. The dog had better figure out how to hook her own leash up and take herself for a walk.

The call was scheduled for 10 a.m. so I woke up at 4:30 in the morning and began my silent vigil of sweating through my sleep pants and telling everyone in earshot that I had a very important business call approaching so they all needed to occupy themselves because for the next five and a half hours I would be preparing for the event.

"Preparing" meant sitting at my desk, staring at the wall and imagining all the different ways I might make a fool of myself on this phone call. Did I understand social media enough to have an intelligent conversation about it? Would that thing happen where I got too nervous and all of the spit in my mouth would dry up leaving me impossibly parched and coughing into the receiver? Did I even remember how to answer the phone? Should I say, "Hi Mark?" Or just "Hello?" as if I hadn't been sitting stock-still for the past five hours clutching my phone waiting for it to ring.

The added stress of not having retained any information from our last meeting due to the chin hair debacle was weighing me down.

The phone rang at exactly 10 a.m. and I was ready for it. "Hi Mark," I croak-screamed upon answering. He didn't seem to notice my weird salutation so that was good I guessed. Thankfully he gave me a recap on last week's conversation and we moved on nicely from there.

"So Lindsay, here's the thing. I'm going to need you to be all in on this because it's just us for now. Do you have other work obligations?" Mark asked.

"I'm doing my online writing, but I can keep up with that in my off hours. I'm also doing casual work at Lethbridge Event Rentals, in the laundry room, but it's only a few days a week so I don't think that will get in the way."

"Okay great, let's get started then."

It was at that point I heard an enormous crashing sound coming from the kitchen. Mark heard it too.

"What was that? Is everything okay over there?" he asked.

"I don't know," I said.

"Well do you need to put me on hold and go check it out?" he asked.

"Yeah that's a good idea."

I ran to the kitchen, where shards of glass littered the linoleum. Soph was perched on the countertop, afraid to make any additional sounds knowing that I was on my very Important business call. As soon as she saw me, she burst into tears.

"Sorry Mom, I dropped the glass," she wailed.

I told Mark I'd call him right back and helped Soph off the counter then cleaned up the glass. Feeling the pressure to get back on the phone with Mark and continue our conversation, I called him immediately, not paying Sophie any more attention.

Two minutes back into our conversation, I was interrupted again by a soft knocking on the door.

"I'm so sorry Mark, can you just hold on one second," I said. I opened the door with such fury that my nine-year-old's eyes visibly widened upon seeing my face. Scared to silence, she held out her hand to reveal a bloody gash—assumably procured during the epic glass shattering fiasco minutes before.

"Oh god, Soph are you okay?" I cried.

"What's wrong, is she okay?" Mark asked from the other end of the line, genuine concern in his voice.

"Uh yeah," I said, trying to decipher if this was an emergency room visit scenario. As I ran Sophie's hand under cold water to wash away the blood, she screamed with the same kind of spirit one might exert while getting waterboarded for intel by a shadowy government agency.

Meanwhile, I was telling Mark that everything was fine and to continue talking about our long term goals for the company and, could he tell me again what the mission statement was?

Just as I was finishing up with Sophie's hand, confident in the knowledge that it was more of a scare and less of a stitches situation, Mark said, "I feel like you've got a lot of stuff going on right now. How about we revisit this in a few days?"

You don't understand, I wanted to say. I blocked out my calendar for this. I tried. But when it comes to motherhood, there's no such thing as blocking out the calendar. Instead, I agreed and hung up the phone. Soph and I cuddled on the couch for a while and I thought about whether this job would be the one for me.

I received an email from Mark a few days later, explaining that he had decided to go in another direction with the business. He was going to put the project on the back burner for a while and he'd call me when he got it up and running again.

Two years later I am still waiting for that call.

Forty-Six

This ever-present fear I have is a silly thing, but silly never meant less frightening. At least for me, it never has. The fear swells when I receive a notification on my work scheduling app saying there's to be a staff get-together happening the following weekend.

I ignore the message, as I do with everything I don't want to acknowledge. Ignoring things I don't want to deal with has always worked well for me. That is, if "working well" means living with a constant, relentless drumming in my chest that remains until the time whatever it is that I am stressing out about happens or I get the guts to deal with the thing I am stressing out about before it happens. The latter rarely occurs. Have I mentioned that procrastination is my sweet spot?

The relentless drumming gets ever heavier whenever someone says, "Hey, so are you coming on Sunday?" while I'm feeding linens through the press or throwing a load of hotel bedsheets into the industrial-sized washing machine.

My boss is one of my favourite people in the world. It's rare to work for someone you can call a true friend, but I am lucky enough to be doing just that.

I was friends with David before I worked for him. When Jamie and I closed the shop, David was kind enough to ask both of us to come work at his event rentals business. I've been working there casually ever since. Jamie works for David whenever he gets laid off from the railroad—which is more often than one might imagine. David has been there for my family so much these past few years.

I hesitantly said I'd be there when David asked if I was coming to the staff party. Usually, I make some sort of excuse for these types of social get-togethers. Excuses like, "Oh, sorry, can't make it, I have to work," but clearly, there are issues with this kind of response regarding staff parties.

There will be many people there. Small talk will need to be made. People will expect normality from me and I cannot promise I will be able to deliver. It will be awkward, and I'm going in solo.

I met David through a mutual friend ten years ago. Look, I don't know if it was ten years ago, but I'm pretty sure it was somewhere around there. At the time, we didn't even live in the same city. Jamie and I were young parents living in Sylvan Lake. Our friend Scott told us he was coming over with a friend. I had been working in the garden all morning—at the time of first meeting David, I was covered in dirt, wearing ratty boxer shorts as gardening gear and looking impossibly dishevelled.

If you knew David, you'd understand why this was a problem. David is one of the most put-together people you'll ever meet. He always looks exemplary and seemingly has never been flustered in his life. Of course, he has been flustered, but he is excellent at not seeming flustered in flustering situations. He masks his flusteredness impeccably with his friendly smile and outgoing attitude.

I was my weird self, flitting around my kitchen offering wine at 11 a.m. and wondering why I can never manage to be a normal human being around people I don't know. I assumed I'd never see the guy again in my life. Partly because I had made such a terrible first impression and partly because we lived in different cities. Then five years later, we moved to the same city as David, and he became a regular at our sandwich shop. Over the years, despite my strangeness, we got to know David more and grew a friendship.

So yes, I'm fortunate to call my boss a friend. I shouldn't be worried about attending a social gathering with friends. Then again, I'm the kind of person who gets nervous about going to my hometown for a long weekend because my bed and toilet are not in my immediate future, so there's that. And yes, I'm working on these issues in therapy, but, as we all know, it takes time. Time that I do not have.

A huge part of me has been conjuring up all kinds of non-work-related excuses for Sunday's event.

- I have family coming to town.
- My shed is on fire.
- My dog is getting an academic award at doggy daycare, and I cannot miss the ceremony. That would be rude.

I've got excuses coming out of my hoo-haw. Because, of course, that's where all good excuses come from. Last night, as I was lounging on my couch fretting about all the things I have no control over, David texted me a meme that said:

The best friendships are with the people you can be dumb af with, and 5 minutes later, you can be having an extremely deep conversation with.

Now let me paint you a little picture of how deep my insecurities run: I read this meme that was sent without any context whatsoever, and the first thing that came to my mind was, *Oh, he probably sent this to the wrong person. He didn't mean to send it to me.* I thought this even though just that day, the two of us were singing loudly in the warehouse about the beauty of having just enough white round tablecloths to fill a last-minute order and then, two minutes later, were seriously talking about how important it was to be true to oneself.

We do this all the time. Singing loudly, dancing bad jigs and having meaningful conversations in weird nonsensical accents. Yet I still wondered if this meme was meant for me. It takes some deep-seated fuckery to have this little self-confidence. I texted him back, saying this was why he was one of my favourite people.

He replied, "I saw this meme and immediately thought of you!"

Forty-Seven

I've said it before, and I'll say it again: I am not a climber. Okay, I've never said that before. But I've thought it for sure. The weird thing is I should be a climber. Being short (I clock in at a whooping 5'1), you'd think I'd have learned how to climb with grace and stealth out of sheer necessity. Not so.

My lack of lower (and let's face it) upper body strength does not lend itself to climbing. Whenever I find myself faced with a precarious situation like being stuck in a tree or on a rock cliff, my arms tremble and immediately turn to jelly. Cards on the table; I've never found myself on a rock cliff. And do you want to know why? Because I'm smarter than that! There's no reason for me to venture out to a rock cliff. All in all, I'm a flat-ground kind of gal.

Except sometimes, we find ourselves in situations we never expected. My work as a laundry wench is usually filled with fresh linen scent and trying to calm down the occasional angry grandmother who swears to the good Lord Jesus that her antique linen napkins got mixed up with ours at her grandson's wedding. (I have yet to find the antique linen napkins but did manage to appease the grandmother by promising to scour our stock until I locate the hallowed items in question.) And sometimes I must partake in the dreaded loading and unloading process.

This entails backing a large truck up to the loading dock and hauling five hundred chairs aboard. And sometimes, the truck operator backs up too close to the wall making it virtually impossible to lower his loading ramp. Which causes me to have to jump onto ground level on the loading dock. Then once we figure out the problem, I watch in horror as my fellow investigators efficiently do this fucking hop/jump/lower body strength move onto the tailgate of the very tall truck and back into the warehouse.

A cold sweat overtakes me. I, too, must now do the hop/jump/lower body strength move to get into the warehouse. That, or look like the fool who has to walk the entire loading dock length and use the door. Pfft. Who even uses doors when you can make a hop/jump/lower body strength move! It seemed pretty straightforward when Susie did it. I can do this. I can hop, jump and lower body strength myself back into the warehouse. I pump myself up mentally. Time is moving very slowly now, and I suspect that the driver of the very large truck is wondering why the hell I'm not moving outta the way. HOLD YOUR DAMN HORSES, GUY. I'M PUMPING MYSELF UP HERE! Getting my foot onto the truck's bumper is not the problem. The problem is hoisting the girth of my body up to the truck's level. Then comes the hop over to the loading dock.

I succeed in the most basic sort of way. I am physically incapable of doing this in a smooth and sophisticated manner, so rather than a hop/jump move, I perform a hoist/waddle/roll extravaganza. I hoist myself onto the truck the way a crane carefully lifts a 700-pound corpse from a bed that's been there for years. I then attempt to step to the loading dock and fail immediately, realizing that my stumpy legs will not stretch that far. The thought occurs that I could live out the rest of my days on this truck bumper, but I quickly dismiss it because the driver sort of creeps me out.

I waddle close enough for my knee to make contact, pray the gods will assist me in my quest and roll my entire body onto the safe and secure ground.

Susie kindly ignores my pathetic attempt at physical activity and avoids eye contact. For that, I am thankful.

Forty-Eight

A strange man in threadbare clothing is sitting alone at a table, and we are all wondering where he came from. So far, I've had no less than seven of my coworkers approach me, asking if I know who the guy is. I don't blame them for wondering because in a classy joint like this, the dude sticks out like a sore thumb.

Our annual staff party is being held at the Norland Estates, and I feel extremely out of place here. Maybe that's why people keep asking me if I know the grubby guy in the corner. Maybe they think we came together. His hair, like mine, is light brown and straggly. He's skinny to my chunky, but we both are wearing jeans with holes in the upper leg area, except mine are intentional, and I get the feeling this guy was recently in some sort of scuffle with a large jungle cat. He's downing a beer, checking out the scene, and at this moment, I very badly wish I hadn't turned down the two drink tickets I was offered when first arriving at the party.

I'm trying to be a better human than I was yesterday. Yesterday, I would have drank all the alcohol I could get my hands on when delving into this kind of social situation. I would have been snozziled good and proper before they even brought out the appetizers because talking to people I know and love is difficult, but this particular staff party doesn't only consist of my coworkers but also our sister company's employees as well. There are a ton of people here, and I am expected to mingle with all of them.

The thing is, I don't want to be the kind of person who needs booze to shmooze, so I decide, on a whim, to hop on the wagon and go without.

I'm sitting at a table with Susie, who is a few coolers deep, and listening to some random dude tell me about his love for skateboarding. It's like his major goal in life is to be Tony Hawk. Or the main attraction in an Avril Lavigne song circa 2002. Wait. What's this now? He's morphed his Ted Talk into how he was thrown out of his house as a teenager.

"I've been making my own way for years now. Don't get me wrong, I love my parents. I just never go and see them anymore."

Yikes.

Susie, the mother saint she is, pays rapt attention to everything this kid says. "Ah, that's so interesting," she says pretty convincingly. But I know Susie, and it's clear to me she doesn't give a shit about skateboarding or this dude's sudden abandonment as a teen. How does she do it? How can she feign interest in the minutia?

I decide to intervene.

"Seriously though? Who is that guy in the corner over there? I've talked to a few people about him, and nobody has seen him before."

We all look over at the guy and get caught staring a little too long. He gives us a nod, which makes us break our gaze and go back to talking about teenage-woes and the wonders of *skater boys*.

I want to tell Susie and this guy whose name I can't remember about the time I was six and woke up to find what looked to be five slimy mouse babies between my legs. At the time, I could, more often than not, be found sleeping in the enormous king-sized bed we had randomly set up in our unfinished basement. This was before all the trauma I now associate with cellar dwellings. Our cat Kia would often lay between my legs and sleep with me for the night. Did I understand the cat was pregnant? I mustn't have because upon waking to find those blood-soaked mewing creatures between my legs, I was positive I had given birth to them myself.

Oh no, I thought, *Mom's going to kill me when she sees I've pooped out rats and ruined the duvet!*

It was a perplexing time to be alive. I don't know how long it took for my surprised cries to morph into screaming, but when my dad finally got downstairs, I was beside myself with new mother fear. "I...I don't know where they came from!" I wailed, fearing, I guess, my life would never be the same now that I had entered into parenthood at six years old.

"Oh look," Dad cooed with the kind of fatherly sigh I had never witnessed from him before. "Kia had her babies."

Kia was nowhere in sight and it occurred to me she had ditched me with this litter of kittens. If she thought I was going to raise these babies of hers, she had another thing coming.

Just as I am about to make the connection between Noname's parents abandoning him and my childhood cat abandoning her young as well, Brenna, a former coworker of ours, approaches our table saying, "Hey did you notice that guy sitting over there?"

"Yeah we were all wondering who he was," I say.

"Turns out he's an escapee from the detox center down the road. He hopped the fence, saw a party going on, and was given a couple of free drink tickets as soon as he walked in. He's been drinking here for over an hour."

Forty-Nine

Did I forget how to talk with strangers? I wondered as I attempted to pour an Irish Red with the perfect amount of head foam. I'm actually fantastic at pouring beer, which is surprising because I'd never poured a professional beer in my life until I offered to volunteer at my favourite local brewery. I had been enjoying that same Irish Red a few weeks prior while my pal and owner of the joint, Kelti, was telling me about how tired she was lately.

We met Kelti and the Theoretically Brewing team a few years back when we owned the Hot Wire and did some promotional events together. Hot-pressed sandwiches and locally crafted beer go together like lipstick and leopard print. Since closing our shop, Jamie and I have tried to get down to the brewery as much as possible to support our fellow small biz friends.

I perhaps had a few too many reds sloshing around in my belly when I said, "Kelti, why don't you train me? I can give you a hand on busy nights!"

Kelti, knowing that I am well versed in the small business world and counter service life, leapt at my offer. "Yes. Let's do that!"

Except it had been four long years since I owned a business or worked in the service industry. For the past four years, I've been holed away in my tiny office writing cringtastic stories. And, of course, the rest of my time is spent in an industrial laundry room, incanting spells over spunk-stained bedsheets.

Hocus pocus, jizzum and sleaze, remove this splooge stain as fast as you please!

As I poured perfect beers for the brewery's International Women's Day Brew launch (see, I told you they were a very cool business), I realized I could be better at conversing with the public. At least I had the wherewithal to refrain from telling the story of when I gave birth to mouse-babies at six years old.

I'd like to think I was being awkward in a lovable way, but I don't think that was the case. Actually, I'm positive that wasn't the case. Whenever I'm in a behind-the-counter scenario, serving human beings, my kneejerk reaction is to get very loud and overuse the phrases "that's hilarious" and "very cool" to such an extent that these two phrases morph into my only known vocabulary.

How the hell did I do this when I used to work behind a counter for a living? How could a few short years allow me to forget my customer service skills?

I was beginning to have a total mental panic attack while pouring a Salty Mavin (previously mentioned Women's Day Brew) for a new customer while loudly saying, "Very cool," to nothing and nobody at all, when both Kelti and I were startled by a tremendous crashing bang coming from the tasting room.

The bar, where me and Kel were pouring beers, and the tasting room, where the bang came from, are separated by a thick wall. We looked at each other in stunned silence. Then the silence broke when the entire tasting room broke out in ominous sighs of, "Ohhhh no!" and "Are you okay?"

We ran to the back. There stood our evening's entertainment: a singer with a broken guitar in her hand and a look of pure defeat on her face.

"What happened?" Kelti asked. I knew enough to understand my go-to lexicon of "very cool" and "that's hilarious" would be inappropriate in this situation, so I willed myself to stay quiet.

"I tripped and fell. Landed on my guitar." The girl looked shattered. I'm not sure how old she was, but I'd be surprised if she were eighteen. She was taking the disastrous situation like a champ, though. The young performer excused herself to the washroom, and that's when everyone in that tiny brewery jumped into action.

"Okay, we need to track down another guitar," said someone.

"I've got one at my house," a girl answered.

"I'll text Jay and see if she can bring an extra," Kelti offered. "She's our second show tonight and due to be here in 20 minutes or so."

Everyone was on their phone, texting and calling, ensuring the show would go on.

The singer came out front, where Kel and I were back pouring beers for the patrons. She was laughing it off. I was astounded at her resilience. I would be a puddle of humiliated tears by this point. That was one amazing kid.

The singer signed the broken guitar, and Kelti planned to hang it on the brewery's wall—a true rockstar if I've ever seen one.

A new acoustic was procured. The show, indeed, went on.

By 8 p.m., I found myself in the tasting room enjoying the music and truly not worrying about being surrounded by a room full of strangers. I thought about community and the weird and lasting webs we weave simply from existing beside one another. My shyness and difficulty conversing with the public have always been there, but I remember that with practice, I can quell the social anxiety that crashes into my brain when confronted with swarms of people.

Life is worth feeling uncomfortable once in a while. Because if all it takes is a bit of awkwardness to grow a network like that around you, then please, accept my "very cools" and I shall bask in the warm embrace of a community.

Fifty

Isn't it always a brisk fall afternoon when it comes to your attention that you're a dirty rotten pervert? For me, this information did not come as a surprise because I have scumbag tendencies. A cute, adorable scumbag to be sure, but a scumbag nonetheless. That's how I've gotten as far as I have in life.

Yet again I was trying out jobs the same way I used to haunt grungy little second hand stores and try on fur coats with cigarette burns in them. Much like the coats, I knew these positions had no future, but seeing how far I'd take it was an interesting social experiment. Like that one time I bought a fluffy faux fur overcoat that was fluorescent orange and I walked around twinning with Gossamer from Looney Toons for, like, six months straight.

The issue was this: I had placed a multitude of nondescript penises on a children's food menu that I designed. Was it intentional? No. I am not some sicko looking for kicks in gross and depraved ways. It was quite the opposite. Apparently, I can't spot a penis when it's right in front of my face.

I was working as a content creator for a local diner. My bosses, Liv and Sandra, were fun and talented people to work for. Their restaurant was successful, and I had been floored six months before when they approached me asking if I'd start doing the social media work for their business. Sandra was getting run down, running the restaurant as well as doing all the online advertising and thought it would be best to begin hiring out for that position. They had both seen the work I'd done for the Hot Wire and enjoyed the humorous spin I'd put on my advertising campaigns. Since I had a fair bit of experience in the food and beverage industry and advertising for such, I didn't hesitate before agreeing to work with them.

A few months after I had begun, Liv asked me if I'd like to redesign her menu. *Yes, I can do that!* I texted her excitedly. I was eager to have the opportunity to show off my budding skills in graphic design. Sure, I had never technically designed a menu, but how difficult could it be?

I used my go-to design program as a starting point but threw in my own unique style. I found easily legible fonts that drew the eye. I splashed pops of colour here and there, and I edited the shit out of that thing. Then I found a cartoony smiling face in the clip art and plopped it down on an artfully drawn cup on the kid's menu.

Except evidently, the nose of that face looked exactly like a flaccid penis.

To me, the picture appeared to be a cute cartoon face on a child's cup. Good and good. I sent it in and Liv and Sandra were happy. They printed off a shwack of menus to distribute in the restaurant.

Later, I got a message from Liv.

"Soooo just had a customer point this out to me," a close-up of the cup's face pinged onto my phone's screen. "Are you trying to put me out of business? Lol."

I don't know if I am really naive or just plain out of touch with what a dick looks like, but I stared at that pic for a good five minutes trying to figure out what was wrong with it.

With a dick-sullied menu in hand, I abashedly made my way to the diner. Upon entry, the server immediately said, "Oh, are you here to talk with Liv about the menu?"

"Yes. Yes, I am," I said, head hanging in shame.

Luckily, we ended up laughing about the entire situation. I will forever be grateful to Liv and Sandra for their graciousness that time I stuck a dong on their menu. After we talked about what could be done about the situation, they fed me free of charge, and upon leaving, I realized I had no cash to tip the server. Please refer to my previous scumbag reference.

When I got home, I passed along the pic to a Facebook group chat I had with my girlfriends and asked, "Does this look like a dick to you guys?" Immediately without even so much as a pause to investigate the picture, they all responded, "Yep, that's a big ole dick on that cup's face."

Interesting. I messaged Liv and asked again if she wanted me to remake the menu. She laughed it off and said it wasn't a big deal. I was dubious.

"Buuuuut, there's a dink on your kid's menu?"

"We've already printed off a bunch of the menus, so I don't want to waste them. But full disclosure; I'm telling everyone that my pervo menu designer snuck a dick on the kid's menu."

Fifty-One

Today, as Susie and I process hundreds of teal and lagoon-coloured napkins through the press, all I can talk about is how bad that comedian was last night. I want to stop talking about it because, as if I'm having an out of body experience, I have lifted out of my physical form and am now hovering outside myself, looking down on my own incoherent ramblings. I sound like a jackass.

I can't stop thinking about how I was heckling the guy. I guess it wasn't so much heckling but instead telling my own much funnier jokes to my table about how unfunny this supposed comedian was.

This guy didn't know how to read the room. He kept making weird references to the LGBTQ community despite their presence in the room. He wasn't so much offensive but instead just really awkward—not in the cute and charming way. He was yelling at people who were getting up after dinner to go for a smoke. He seemed uninterested in his own material.

I was loudly joking about how my vagina had gotten more laughs in the past week than this guy, and the people sitting at my table were laughing which always encourages me. Although David has made it very clear he doesn't want to hear about the adventures of my whisker biscuit, he still was more amused by my impromptu vagina inspired spoken word poetry than anything this bro on the stage was saying.

What is it about this mediocre performer that riled me up so much? Was it his shitty delivery of lacklustre material? Or more likely, am I jealous?

From the time I was thirteen years old, Dad said (with no hint of humour in his voice), "I'd say it's about time you go out and find yourself a job, Lester. I can't be paying for your stuff for the rest of my life." I've been hard at work ever since.

Over the years, I found employment as a cashier, fried chicken slinger, daycare provider, housekeeper, telephone operator, clown, business owner, and warehouse worker. All while writing my little heart out and gaining as much experience and rejection in the biz as possible. Maybe I couldn't afford more than a few general studies courses at our local community college, but I could damn well get the hands-on experience I needed to move my writing forward.

And here I am, doing nothing with that experience. I'm complaining about a guy who, maybe didn't give us his best show but at least had the balls to get up on that stage and put himself out there. I've become my worst nightmare: someone who pinpoints everyone else's shortcomings but can't see her own.

I'm a wannabe writer. I'm scared to the point of inaction. I've turned my back to the keyboard so as not to burden myself with the horror of a silent audience. I refuse to take a leap in any direction for fear of the rejection that could come tumbling down. Maybe it's the cold-hearted farm kid in me—that little girl standing on a mountain of potatoes while punching her dad directly in the face because he decided to scare her in a pitch-dark cellar—but I have no sympathy for myself or the bad comedian. I need to get my shit together and write something of value, do something of value, and the guy on stage needs to come up with some better material.

Fifty-Two

When the COVID-19 quarantine hit, a tiny online community lent me the bravery to believe in my writing again. Jamie and I were laid off from our jobs, but I had found my stride doing online writing and humour work. The pandemic scared me because sickness and disease scare me. But isolation and stay-at-home orders? I was totally down for that.

To outsiders looking in, I appeared to be the most loyal citizen on the planet, obeying every government plea to avoid get-togethers and remain six feet apart from people at the grocery store. Really though, I was overjoyed to do these things. Solitude is my safe place. Alone with a computer is where I yearn to be ninety percent of the time.

Now I was alone with a computer, my three most important people locked up in the house safe and sound with me, with the added benefit of actually having time to make some money with this writing thing.

In the past, non-creatives would smirk when I told them I was a writer. I don't know why they did this. Maybe it was because up to this point, as far as books went, I had self-published exactly two tomes. Well, they weren't precisely tomes; instead, they were closer to one-hundred-page glimpses into this ever-anxious brain that has little to no patience with the publishing industry.

I hired a vanity press to publish my poetry in 2011. Ten out of ten, do not recommend. Then in 2019, I self-published a book of short fiction called

Incompetent Overlords—A Collection of Strange Stories. Although most people who bought the book were friends and family, I received exactly zero rave reviews.

Now, I was becoming popular for my online humour work. I wrote personal narratives about life, mental health, and occasionally shitting myself. It was humble work.

Many folks in my life didn't get the whole blogging thing. They'd hesitate to tell me stories because they knew I'd turn around and write about them. They'd ask me, "Why can't you write fiction, Lindsay? It would be so much safer for everyone involved." But that was a stupid question considering these were the same people who refused to give me rave reviews on my fiction.

As I delved deeper into writing platforms, I began meeting fellow writers. Casual comments led to Facebook messaging, and eventually, a couple of the more adamant writers I befriended wore me down and convinced me to do video chats with them. To this day, awaiting a Zoom call sends a bolt of anxiety through me strong enough to cramp my toes and set my molars on edge. Something about answering the call and not knowing if my microphone will work or if my camera is angled just right to show off my double chins causes the fear to explode deep in my belly.

There were about twenty of us who started our own little Facebook group page and there we would share our writing, ask for advice and make weird inappropriate jokes that were wildly hilarious because writers are funny people.

Whenever the monotony of homeschooling the kids or having to handwash another bag of groceries got me down, I'd turn to my writer's group for a pick-me-up. And that's exactly what they did, they picked me up.

For years, I thought writing was a solitary act. That's why I chased after the career so fervently. I could blog my little stories and publish them and then exactly zero people would read them. Done and done. Then, without warning, these kind, thoughtful, and incredibly talented people from all over the world flooded my online life, and I wondered how I had spent so many years writing alone.

Writing may be solitary but exercising our creativity, flexing our editorial muscles and submerging ourselves in the written word is anything but. This group of people whom I'd probably never meet in real life were the first to congratulate me when I'd place in various writing contests. They were always willing to look at writing drafts I wasn't sure about, and they'd cheer me on when that familiar angst of self-doubt overtook me. Being a part of a community like this taught me how to appreciate people again.

Fifty-Three

For the first time in a very long time, I could buy a new pair of shoes and not feel guilty about it.

When we opened our sandwich shop in 2016, we had the world by the short and curlies. Well, that's at least what we thought. "I," long pause, "am a business owner," I'd say proudly to people when they'd ask me what I did for a living.

"Oh wow!" They'd reply because, for some reason, people hold entrepreneurs in high esteem. You could be the owner of a squirrel breeding facility set on bringing down Big Energy with your army of power grid infiltrating rodents, and people would still think you're the savviest business professional on the face of the planet. Actually, I sort of would love to own that business.

Meanwhile, I'd be slinging sandwiches and thinking about my overdrawn bank account. The world of business ownership isn't always what it's cut out to be. After closing our shop, we set out on the long road to financial recovery, which meant paying down the debt we had acquired and never again eating out at a restaurant because food prices are forever skyrocketing.

My family had been living on a shoestring budget. The people in our lives marvelled at how we survived, but my husband and I knew the truth. You just got on with it. You paid the bills or called the bill companies and told them you couldn't pay them that month. That's life. We managed to make some headway, though. With Jamie working on the railroad and me scrubbing laundry while also gaining a few wins in the writing biz, we finally saw some green coming in. Well, as Canadians, we finally saw some blue, purple and sometimes green, coming in.

We had a bit of money in the bank. I still didn't pay my bills on time but that wasn't because I didn't have the cash. Rather, I liked to hoard the money in my chequing account and open my app about ten times a day to see it in there. Having a dollar amount that doesn't have a minus sign in front of it was a novel experience.

The cheapskate mentality we had lived by for the past five years wasn't easy to let go. Even with the extra funds, I still purchased discount meat from the store and looked for deals anywhere I could. Then one day, I realized I needed new slip-on shoes. I don't wear shoes very often as I like to feel the gravel beneath my toes.

Slip-ons have always been my favourite type of footwear because as soon as I step onto my property, I can whip them off with great vigour, watch them fly through the air and rejoice in the feeling of the soles of my feet connecting with the earth. The slip-ons I had, though, were getting old. My husband was embarrassed to go anywhere with me because of the holes in the soles. I walk funny and tend to kick my feet backwards and high when ambling about, which meant those travelling behind me could see the holes.

They'd loudly whisper things like, "Oh dear, that woman desperately needs some new shoes," when seeing my footwear. It didn't bother me, but Jamie cares about this sort of thing and told me I deserved new shoes.

So, I set out to Walmart. I knew luck was on my side when I spotted black slip-on shoes in the five-dollar discount bin. I bought my five-dollar shoes and slipped them on in the car, feeling fine.

That afternoon, as I was in the dollar store buying discount deodorants for the family, I started smelling something foul. It smelled as though a rabbit had pooped in a rotten banana peel, and the substance was left in the sun to sour. *Huh. That's unpleasant.* I thought while side-eyeing the impeccably dressed woman beside me.

You, my friend, cannot hide your stank behind that expensive façade, I judgmentally reckoned while smirking to myself. I headed over to the greeting card section because I like to buy cards in bulk—so I have a card for every occasion, despite having never, in my life, sent someone a greeting card. The smell followed me. I looked for the well-dressed woman, but she was nowhere to be found.

The smell at this point was so intense that I started gagging. I have a touchy gag reflex that has never served me well in the bedroom aspects of my life. It seemed as though the smell was coming from me. My feet, to be exact.

Traumatic memories flooded my mind's eye as I recalled with great detail yet another time my foot stench was my own demise. Because you see, this was not the first time I had been caught with stinky feet.

After three years working at Lethbridge Event Rentals, David finally allowed me to leave the safe confines of my laundry room.

I was working with Brenna, my supervisor at the time, and we were building a particularly glamorous banquet room complete with forty foot sheer column draping and those super inconvenient but fancy-ass standing tables. We had just begun working on the first column when I caught a whiff.

"Just pull over one of those chairs, and we can stand on that to reach," Brenna said. "Oh but make sure you take your shoes off before you get on the chair because we don't want to get them dirty."

My heart nugget stilled for a split second, "Uh, what now? You need me to take my shoes off?"

"Yeah, I just don't want to risk scuffing up the chairs with our shoes."

"Oh yeah, cool, cool, cool. Of course," I said, sucking the last remaining moisture from my tongue. I don't believe there ever was or ever will be again a time when I moved slower. Locating the chair and painstakingly moving it toward where Brenna stood waiting with a dumbfounded look on her face, I pondered my predicament.

My feet smelled like that dead bird I found in my garden yesterday. I had no idea why this foot funk was hammering down upon me, but there was no time to worry about such trivial matters now.

I'M NOT THE MANAGER HERE

My plan was simple. I would attempt to stay as far away from Brenna as humanly possible and then maybe she wouldn't notice the horrific half-dead-tuna stench radiating from my toesies. This worked for about five minutes. Then Brenna said, "Oh my God, do you smell that?"

"Oh yeah, that's unpleasant." Come on Brown, play it cool, woman.

"I think that's my feet!" Brenna said, looking down at her own shoeless feet.

I nervously laughed and continued to secure white sheer draping to a column in the banquet room. Sure, it was awful of me to let Brenna believe that it was her feet that stunk. And yes, maybe I should have womaned up and stated my truth which would obviously have been, "Nay, my friend, 'tis my bases that bloom with fetid repugnance!" While begging for her forgiveness because what kind of a jerk lets someone believe they smell like something straight out of the depths of Satan's own asshole? Me. I do.

I think Brenna knew all along that it was my feet that were stinking up the joint. But Brenna is a better human than I, so she took the brunt of the stench on herself and instead never asked me to leave the secured confines of my laundry room again.

I look down at these stinky soles and realize that slip-on shoes should probably be worn with socks. But as per my earlier statement, I hate things on my feet and only wear the bare minimum when necessary. These five-dollar shoes had no breathing abilities, and my clammy tootsies were begging for air. Pools of sweat had accumulated in the bottoms of my shoes, creating a sort of stench that threatened to blow the place up at any second. And by "the place," I mean the general vicinity of wherever I was standing. It was getting real bad up in there, you guys. Even children—the stinkiest of all the humans—were beginning to look at me funny when crossing my rancid path.

The woman in the expensive pantsuit strolled by. She gave me a side-eye while bringing her hand up to her face, trying to create a layer of scent protection between my feet and her nostrils. I should have put down my basket full of cheap toiletries and left right then and there. But it was my shopping day, and I didn't want to spend the extra gas to drive home (four blocks), wash my dawgs, find unstinkable shoes and then come all the way (again, four blocks) back to the dollar store.

So, I did what any financially conscious person would do in this situation. I discreetly made my way back to the bathroom supply section of the store. I did a couple of shifty eyes to my left and right to ensure no employees were around. I grabbed a lavender-scented lotion and went to town on my feet.

The result wasn't great.

The rancid smell of sweat-stained soles was strong and now mingling with a very cheap faux lavender atrocity, but you work with what you got when you are in this sort of situation. I wanted to put the industrial-sized vat of floral lotion back on the shelf. It was like, only missing two scoops, for Christ's sake! But, in the end, my better judgement got the best of me. Leaving an opened jar of anything on a shelf for some unsuspecting sucker to buy isn't my style.

I looked down at my feet as I made my way to the register. The smell was improving because the longer this cheap lotion was on my skin, the stronger it got. Now, instead of smelling like a dead fish with maggots crawling out of its eyes, I had the odour of a ninety-year-old woman with a potpourri-filled sachet in her pocket because she couldn't find her perfume and figured, "Meh, who will know the difference anyway?"

Not to mention my feet were covered in big white splotches of lotion. You try to sneak on stolen body cream from the dollar store flawlessly! I guess you're expecting that as soon as I got home, I threw out the shoes that had caused me so much grief. And I suppose that's what I should have done. But unfortunately, I couldn't. I wanted to see if they might be salvageable after a wash.

They weren't. This same situation repeated the following week when I tried to wear them out again. As I stood over the bin in our basement dedicated to "clothes to be donated" (but in reality, it's just a container in our basement that will remain there forevermore), I second-guessed myself again. Maybe, just maybe, I could give them another try.

Fifty-Four

I am sitting at my computer desk, silently sobbing onto a keyboard, frantically looking up Ainslee's email address. Ainslee was a regular at the Hot Wire and one of the first friendly faces I met when moving to Lethbridge.

I know from using my impeccable listening/Facebook creeping skills that Ainslee is a psychologist. I've always enjoyed Ainslee's company. I know that Jamie's benefits from the railroad cover a chunk of mental health services. So I figure there might be a chance that Ainslee can help me with her wizardry if I can gather up the guts to email her.

Sometimes we find ourselves teetering over an edge and don't realize we are falling until both feet have left solid ground. It happens in the fast and hard way, as if one of your sworn enemies snuck up behind you and shoved you off the cliff with no warning. Only a sworn enemy could do such a despicable thing. Too bad I have so many sworn enemies it makes it impossible to narrow down the perp.

The truth is anything can push you over that cliff once you've ventured close enough. Money problems. Family drama. That dude at the Walmart who looked into your basket and saw seven bags of chips and gently directed you to the produce section, which gave you the kneejerk reaction to scream, "There was a sale on, asshole!"

I have been teetering over a cliff edge for a long time now. I don't want to be afraid of new people or experiences. I don't want to feel that dark wash of hopelessness as soon as I open my eyes in the morning. For months, or maybe even years, I've been living on autopilot. Waking up and working on whatever needs to be done, while shoving down the bad feelings and trying my best to just get on with it.

Living with low-grade depression is a thing I did until I couldn't do it anymore. I've felt the sting of anxiety for as many years as I can remember. It was only after closing down our business that I recall feeling the talons of depression creep in. At the time, I assumed a little blueness was expected. We had lost our livelihood. Friends and family agreed, saying a bit of lingering sadness was indeed expected.

So I kept living in the sadness. It finally occurred to me that rather than having a random down day here and there, I couldn't remember having a truly good day. The dread I felt was all-consuming. Minor disputes between family members were eating me alive. I was melting down at work over the tiniest hiccups. I'd miscount a return box and find we were three tablecloths short and fly into a rage. "Why can't people just return their damn items!" Then when Susie would double check my count, finding that all the tablecloths were there, I'd berate myself for being an idiot.

I found little joy in sitting down with my children and talking for hours—an activity we've enjoyed since they were old enough to craft a decent joke. Somedays, when Jamie was at work and we were readying ourselves for bed, I'd find myself with a rare burst of energy and say, "Hey, let's go get a smoothie!" This is the kind of thing the kids and I loved to do. Go grab a cheap treat and sit up late at the kitchen table talking about anything and everything. Lars and Sophie are pro storytellers, and yet...

I kept telling myself I just had to get on with it.

There comes a point when you can no longer live with the sadness or the stress of being human. We get on with it, and get on with it and get on with it some more. Then we crawl into an empty bathtub and curl into the fetal position. We shut ourselves away from the world because "getting on with it" simply doesn't work anymore. So I gathered up some guts and asked for help. Ainslee emailed me back within the day and said she would love to meet with me.

Between the social anxiety that is consuming my life, my ever-expanding depressive state and the helplessness I feel when having to navigate my incessant need to please those around me, I am a blubbering mess as soon as I step into Ainslee's waiting room.

The office reminds me of seashell-lined beaches—all blues and whites with pops of seafoam green here and there. Between sobs, I think, *it's so serene in here.* The windows are covered in distortion glass to block out any looky-loos but still allow light in. I sit on the couch, and before Ainslee can even start, I say, "I don't recognize myself anymore."

Fifty-Five

I have decided I am the warehouse manager of Lethbridge Event Rentals. Of course, I haven't been appointed to the role. David has not thrust this responsibility on me, and no one else involved in the business acknowledges my self-imposed managerial title. I am still but a lowly laundry wench, as far as anyone in the company is aware.

It's strange because, thus far, I've avoided any real employment responsibility. "Sorry, I'm not the manager here," I'd say while slinging chicken in Sylvan Lake when an irate customer would come back seething because they received thighs in their twenty-piece bucket. "Oh, I apologize; I'm actually not the manager here," I'd coolly spout during my housekeeping days in Victoria when a guest would find lipstick on the rim of their in-room coffee cup.

Even when we owned our sandwich shop, when unruly customers would phone and tell me they received food poisoning from a soft pretzel, I'd apologize and let them know I'd pass their complaint on to the manager. Because honestly, who has time for bullshit like that?

So why now, after all this time, am I pretending to be a manager? In my defence, I have been given a slight amount of authority. David is on vaycay with his fiance, leaving Ali and me in charge of the business in his absence. In truth, it's Ali who's in charge. I'm just here to pick up any slack or perform a happy little jig for Ali when things get stressful.

Every morning, I saunter out to the front desk from my laundry room, anxiety dripping off my bleach-soaked hands, bemoaning the undue strain this extra responsibility is placing on my oh-so-weary shoulders. Ali, being the prince he is, sets aside his mountain of paperwork and listens to my woes.

"You're doing fine," he assures me.

And I say, "Really? Do you think so?" and he reiterates, for the twentieth time, that David has faith in me to look after the warehouse, so I should stop fretting so much.

I'm troubled by my new temporary position as warehouse manager because, in truth, I have no idea what is going on in this place. The eighteen-year-old kids I am charged to manage are way more knowledgeable than me in all things event rentals. From what vases are to be used for the Miller wedding to what company we hire for our carpet cleaning needs—I know none of it. More often than not, I find myself asking them thirty questions a day, which kills any confidence I might have had going into this thing.

Susie tells me to fake it till I make it, but that's not my style. I wish it were, but I'm terrible at faking things. I've always found it helpful to wear every emotion on my sleeve and hope that the surrounding people pity me while giving me delicious food and soft hugs.

When I was nineteen and living in a bachelor suite in Red Deer, Alberta, I applied for a manager position at the local Denny's. I imagined my life becoming so much better after receiving the job. Think of the prestige I'd receive when telling people I managed a Denny's. I envisioned my small and humble office, a desk heaped with all the paperwork that a restaurant manager might oversee. The term "boss bitch" hadn't come around yet, but the idea of finally becoming the self-assured woman in business I knew I was deep in my soul was indeed appealing. That's what I thought of when imagining the Denny's manager position—finally, the opportunity to be the boss of something.

That evening, as I smoked a joint with Janelle, I told her I had applied for the manager's position. Janelle looked me in the eyes, taking an extended pull off the doobie. She continued staring at me as she exhaled, thinking long and hard about my announcement. Then in an unexpected turn of events, she began laughing so uncontrollably that she started to hyperventilate.

As is the case when anyone gets a laugh attack in your general vicinity, I, too, started laughing. Oh, how we laughed and laughed at the prospect of me being a Denny's Floor Manager. Finally, after about ten minutes of no words being passed between us, only laughter and the occasional coughing fit, Janelle gasped, "I just can't stop picturing you in your little Denny's button-down and stiff polyester pants." This visual got me going all over again, and it was about that time I realized I didn't want to be the manager of anything.

Not that there's anything wrong with button-downs and stiff polyester pants. I currently own several pairs of button-downs that I've sewn additional pockets into, and that's where I keep my snacks for when I get peckish. Stiff polyester pants? All the better to hide my FUPA. It's not so much the outfit that steers me away from managerial positions but rather the obligation. Once you wear that hallowed hat of responsibility, you must be steadfast in your execution. You are the person who will fix the problems. You are the one who must make the phone calls and attend company meetings. You are the one who can no longer have ICP lyrics as your email signature because some important business person somewhere will see it and be offended because they don't know what a damn Juggalo is. I don't want to be a manager because, at the heart of the thing, it goes against everything I am.

How have I forgotten all this? I wonder as I bossily argue with one of my supposed subordinates about how many shades of taupe napkins we own. I'm not trying to start a fight over napkins. It's just that I'm on edge. Earlier in the day, I nearly sent out the wrong order on the delivery truck because, as previously mentioned, I am terrible at managerial things. I didn't realize my mistake until the delivery driver was climbing into her enormous box truck and about to exit the loading dock. Being on the opposite side of the warehouse, I began screaming, "Wait! Wait—I sent the wrong order!" while waddle-running across the warehouse and waving my arms frantically.

"But at least you caught the mistake," Susie, my built-in cheerleader, reminds me now. It isn't the order mix-up, or the napkin debate, or even the daily injustice of having boys only a few years older than my son roll their eyes at me when I ask for the tenth time in a row to put those fucking chair covers away that's getting me down. It is the innate knowledge creeping up from the nether regions of my brain that I truly am not the manager here.

I think of Dad, always pushing me to work hard and take the opportunities presented to me, and I worry that I'm letting him down in some way by not pursuing this one. I think back on all of the crappy, disgusting blue-collar jobs I've pandered to over the years and find that I remember almost all of them with fondness.

Maybe the end goal isn't working our way up the ladder but instead enjoying the climb. Or, in my case, enjoying sitting on the third rung from the bottom because it's a pretty decent view from there.

Is this my anxiety talking? Am I scared to put myself out there and go for the gold? The prestigious manager position. I think of Janelle telling me all those years ago that she just can't picture me in a manager's uniform without laughing. I don't blame her. Neither can I.

Fifty-Six

Anislee and I talk about my past trauma during our bi-weekly sessions. We do EMDR to relieve some of the pent-up bullshit that lives deep in my brains and bones. I feel stupid and silly and weird when she asks me to roleplay difficult conversations with friends and family from eons ago but visualize them into something positive. At first, it feels ridiculous to pretend, but as time goes on and I get better at roleplaying with my therapist *weird* it starts to become normal.

Ainslee tells me to push past the embarrassment and, like Nike once said, just do it.

I realize that many of the tools she gives me to help ease my anxieties are the same ones Susie would suggest I do when feeling overwhelmed in the laundry room. Within seconds of pretending, the conversation becomes real, and I allow the memories to pour out of me and into this tiny seascape room. My body lightens, and I know that Ainslee is a real-life superhero. Somehow beyond all comprehension, this woman sitting before me can fish out these awful thoughts, memories and feelings that have built up over a hard life and abolish them into oblivion. It's magic.

I came across a perfectly round stone on my walk today. It was weird because I had just glanced down amidst a sea of pebbles on the pathway, and my gaze went directly to this one disk-shaped rock. This intense surge of glee tore through me, and I yelled, "Lucy! Look, a perfectly round stone!"

Lucy, my dog, looked at me dubiously as if saying, "It's just a rock, lady. Let's get moving. I need to pee on that desiccated tree stump over there."

I tried to walk away from it, but something stopped me, and just as a child would, I ran back and plucked the stone up off the ground and shoved it in my pocket.

Once home, I examined the pebble only to find it wasn't perfectly round. There were dents and crannies I previously ignored. On closer inspection, Lucy was right; it was just a damn rock. Why had I gotten so excited about this thing? Yet rather than tossing it out into the backyard, I stuffed it in my pocket again for safekeeping. I couldn't throw it away.

I don't know how young I was when I began to worry about what other people thought of me. Maybe I've always worried about it. We start small, us people pleasers. We work hard to ensure we are the humans our parents, teachers, aunts, and uncles want us to be. We crave that pedestal—there we shall sit pompously, lording it over all the minions beneath us who didn't have the gumption to get perched there themselves.

Only recently did I come to understand that this is what I've been doing my entire life. I don't pander to the needs of others because I genuinely have a good heart and a giving soul. I don't care about helping a stranger. I want the recognition. I crave the dopamine that shoots into my brain-crevices each time someone tells me I'm doing a good job, or that little spontaneous jig was very interesting indeed.

I am a trained monkey looking for her banana treat.

Ainslee doesn't judge me when I tell her I sometimes crave the idea of being selfish. I say it in a way that she probably should judge because "I just don't want to care about other people" is word vomit at its worst. But Ainslee is either a very skilled actress or impeccably trained in her profession. Probably the latter because she tells me it's normal for people-pleasers to want to be selfish sometimes. She tells me that the things I'm feeling are expected, and that is comforting.

I am learning how to be more assertive. I'm learning to please those I genuinely want to please rather than looking for some stilted self-appointed consolation prize for putting others before myself. I'm learning how to live in this awkward skin suit and enjoy the ride.

These realizations are mind blowing. They plant a seed, an imperfect stone, in my head, giving me the confidence to reshape my definition of me.

Fifty-Seven

I attended the Lethbridge Business Awards with my friend and coworker, Alinafe, who manages the front end of Lethbridge Event Rentals. David was away on a much-deserved cruise with his partner so Ali and I went in his stead. I, of course, was palms-sweaty kind of nervous, but because of the work I've been doing in therapy, I managed to avoid bailing out last minute. Bailing is my usual go-to with things that make me nervous. Instead, I pulled on my big girl panties (Spanx) and attended a fancy dinner with Lethbridge's business sector.

When you find yourself in a room full of business professionals, and you are but a lowly laundry wench, it is difficult not to feel second-rate. You think, wait, why am I here in my weird red dress and slightly presidential updo? You start looking at the table linens and silently cursing any guest who spills a drop of wine or grounds crumbs into the ivory coloured fabric. "For the love of polyester, don't use linen napkins to sop up the gravy!" you find yourself whisper-screaming at an overdressed woman in a ballgown.

I was there to support Ali because if we won in our category (Best Employer), Ali was going to have to make a speech on David's behalf. I was planning to tag along and wave importantly to the people because that's what my dress and, more specifically, my hair needed from me.

Alas, we did not win in our category, so now I really didn't know why I was there. I looked at the people seated at our table—everyone was so self-assured and confident. It seems to me that some people must shoot out of their mother's vagina with all the confidence in the world. Or perhaps they were faking it like I was trying to fake it at that moment. Was I doing a better job faking my confidence than I thought? Did I look just as self-assured and awesomely cool as all the other people at that eight-top? Did casually mentioning that I write online articles about cleaning the occasional pool of period blood off bedding make things weird?

I felt a distinct sweat streak forming around the waistband of my underwear. This happens when I get nervous—I sweat right through my panties. It is just as cringy as that last sentence implied. I couldn't decide if I should excuse myself to sop up my panty sweat or if pulling the elastic away from my skin for a split second might help cool things off down there. Unfortunately, I opted for the latter choice. I was not aware that there is a very real and distinct popping fart sound that occurs when you elasti-slap your own gunt. There I was, having just bitched slapped my lower abdomen fat roll with the elastic band of my perspiration-drenched control tops, and looking right into the eyes of Ali's plus one.

Kenny didn't know what to say. I didn't know what to say. I knew that Kenny had heard the slap-fart, and Kenny knew I knew he had heard the slap-fart. How does one breach such a conversational barrier? *Oh, that wasn't a fart—just my very moist underwear band slapping against my equally drenched stomach.*

That's when I noticed I was holding Ali's wine glass up to my mouth. Ahhh shit, leave it to the weird slap-farting chick to grab the wrong glass. Any mentally sound person would have placed it back down and hoped to hell that no one saw. But I was in too deep at that point. I decided it would be better to bring the entire table's attention to my whoopsie daisy by scream-whispering, "Ha! This is your wine, Ali, not mine!"

Ali is as good as they come. He is an actor and singer who performs at least once a year in one of the community theatre productions here in Lethbridge. He's talented and funny. Ali and I enjoy the same sense of humour, but more importantly, we loathe similar things, so we can shit talk for hours. How can a person live without a friend like that? Ali also understands that my brain can be a hot mess sometimes, so he just laughed along at my word vomit and shrugged it off, ignoring my ever-reddening face.

I was not as cultured, confident, or self-assured as any of the people at the awards ceremony. Well, except for that drunk MC who kept telling unfunny jokes and grazing his hand along the female winner's lower backs. If anyone was a hot mess that night, it was that dude.

This feeling of inadequacy was a thing that would have bothered me much more six months ago. I still get uncomfortable. I say weird things and tell even weirder jokes. But I've learned how to love myself for the strange woman I am, rather than try to shrink myself because of it.

The warehouse manager position at work still lingers in the back of my brain. Dangerous notions of what-if begin to pitter patter through my skull box. With this newfound therapy-confidence comes all kinds of possibilities.

The dreaded slap-fart remains unmentioned to this day.

The End

Afterword

There are certain moments in life you can't take back. For example, that one time when I was talking to my neighbour, whom I had never met before, and telling him how much Lucy wanted to meet his new little puppy. I was enthusiastically rubbing the new puppy's belly at the time.

"Oh, Lucy has wanted to meet you for sooooo long," I crooned in the way all dog lovers do when near a four-legged furball. The man, whose name I did not know, smiled awkwardly. After thirty seconds of me reiterating how much Lucy would love to be friends with his little puppers, I noticed my neighbour backing away slowly while attempting to pull his dog with him. It seemed weird that he was being so weird, but people in general are weird, so I just went with it.

As I was walking home, it occurred to me that if I didn't know my neighbour's name, he probably didn't know my name. Much less my dog's name (Lucy). Wait. Did he think I was referring to myself when saying, "Oh, Lucy has wanted to meet you for sooooo long," but in the third person? How many times did I say that in our brief encounter? Probably too many.

Did he imagine me staring out my living room window as he carried the new pup into his home, rubbing my hands together maniacally while say' cutesy baby voice, "New doggo for Lucy to love?"

Creepy.

So now my neighbour thinks I'm this canine-obsessed psychopath who refers to herself in the third person. How am I supposed to rectify that? Whenever I see him getting into his car or walking the dog, I want to call out to him, "Oh, hi! Just so you know, Lucy is my dog. I'm Lindsay. Remember that time over a year ago when I was referring to Lucy? That was my dog, not me. I don't refer to myself in the third person. Well, not often anyways." I never bellow this convoluted statement out to the neighbourhood because I fear that would only perpetuate the strangeness of the situation. So the neighbour and I remain nonverbal acquaintances who are slightly wary of one another.

This little tale is a lesson in why you should never name animals with human names and, as stated earlier, how some things you simply can't take back.

Six months ago I was sitting in a small meeting room with David. I was passionately ranting about issues I had been noticing while working. Minor problems with the division of labour and work tasks weren't being delegated evenly throughout the staff. Some employees were feeling discontented, verging on disgruntled. People were coming to me with their problems, which was odd because I thought I had made it perfectly clear that I was just the laundry wench up in this bitch. I had no idea what to do about it so I called a meeting with the boss man.

By this point in our relationship, reader, I feel that you understand at your core how terrible I am at dealing with stressful situations in a professional manner. Once again my passionate ranting morphed into crying. Except I wasn't ashamed of the crying this time. I used my gushing emotions to anchor myself in what I knew deep down was inevitable.

For over a year, David has been gently trying to convince me to take the manager position in the warehouse. From dropping subtle hints like, "Hmmm, I wonder who we should hire for the manager position," while making intense eye contact with me, to less subtle hints like, "Lindsay, when are you going to be ready to take this position?" For over a year, I have politely told him, "Over my dead body."

I started writing a book called "I'm Not the Manager Here." That's how vehemently adamant I was about not becoming the manager of that place.

The thought of overseeing warehouse operations for a business dealing with enormous wedding and decor accounts sent chills of inadequacy up my spine. I can barely organize my underwear drawer, let alone ensure the safe delivery of decor for a $6000 event.

The same fear that has plagued me my entire life continued to stack bricks between me and any future growth. Little did the fear know I was coming for it.

I had months of regular therapy sessions under my belt. Over the past six months, I had learned how to steadily disassemble the negative self-talk that had stopped me from progressing. I put to rest the shame and guilt I had been carrying around from the experiences I survived during those formative years. I learned how to embrace the fear rather than hide from it.

I was finally ready to smash through that brick wall like the badass Kool-Aid Man I was.

As I sobbed on a lonely chair in a tiny office, hoping my tears came off as badass Kool-Aid Man, I blurted out, "Look, I think I'm ready to take on more responsibility."

To say I hadn't been thinking about accepting the manager position would be a lie. Over the previous months, as staff members trickled into my laundry room telling me their woes, I'd look out at our expansive warehouse and ideas—terrible, hideous ideas—were beginning to take shape. Maybe I could implement an employee rewards system for a job well done. How hard could the organization be for the outgoing and returned orders? I've always enjoyed making lists, and that's not a far stretch from an Excel spreadsheet, right?

As I said the words, David's eyes lit up. "Do you think you're ready for that?"

A year ago, when the thought of being in charge of staff, events, timesheets, and all the rest came up, a small piece of my soul withered into a pile of petrified dust. Now, beside that pile of dust was a small nugget of excitement. Somehow the fear of not enough had transformed into a quiet confidence that whispered, "Fuck ya, you can do this, Lindsay."

I'm well underway in my management training, having learned all sorts of organizational tips and tricks to keep the warehouse running smoothly. Sometimes I feel the doubt of "not enough" creep in, but just as quickly, I vanquish those thoughts by loudly yelling *you got this, my friend!*

As I wade through these managerial waters, there are good and bad days. Some days I feel like I'm drowning. Many days I feel like crying—and then I do cry, and it feels great to get it out of me. Most days though, despite the added responsibility, I feel lighter without that load of fear holding me down.

Acknowledgements

Years ago, when writing a book first tiptoed onto my radar, I assumed the job would be a one-woman task. I reckoned I'd breeze through crafting the stories, run that sucker through an online editing service, and shove it out into this big imperfect world.

Instead of all that, completing this book took hundreds of hours for me and others to bring it to fruition. As mentioned in chapter fifty, I no longer consider writing a solitary job. I am so grateful to all those who invested their time, energy and positive vibes into this book. It is a testament to the beauty of connection and togetherness.

I'm Not the Manager Here would still be a messy, unorganized Word doc if not for the developmental genius of my editor, Danielle Loewen. She transformed a compilation of haphazard essays into a living, breathing memoir.

Thank you, Danielle, for your hard work and for lending me your mastery of the written word to soak up while editing this book.

Thank you to David, Ali and the LER team.

I know how brutal it must have been for the past couple of years listening to me talk nonstop about "my book" and the unending struggles accompanying such an endeavour, but you persevered. And look, now you're characters in a published book! So, uh, that's gotta count for something, right? Seriously though, there would be no story without this business and you beautiful humans, and I thank the laundry gods often for bringing us all together.

Aimée Gramblin, a fellow writer I met through Medium.com, was a nonstop support system in the early days of writing I'm Not the Manager Here. She provided unwavering moral support and somehow managed to nudge me out of my comfort zone enough to convince me to do a few Zoom calls with her.

Aimée, you have one of the most beautiful souls out there, which is why your eyes were the first to read these words. Your initial critiques were constructive yet always kind—exactly what I needed then. Thank you so so much, my friend.

A big thanks to my family, who also endured countless conversations about story structure, book covers and other writing jargon. Honestly, though, I'm not too sorry for that because both Lars and Sophie gave me a couple of great one-liners for the book, and Jamie was a steady source of hilarious material.

I will probably keep bugging you guys with writing stuff since you're all creative brainiacs.

A big thanks to all those who gave input and feedback on the many book cover ideas I spewed all over Facebook.

The most enormous thanks to my co-laundry wench, Susie.

Susie, Susie, Susie. This book would not exist without you. You reminded me how vital my writing was every day. Your resiliency and kindness are unmatched, and I am forever grateful that our paths intertwined in this hectic, extraordinary life.

And a huge thank you to my readers.

Your comments, feedback and laughter continue to give me the confidence to move forward.

To my biggest fan of all, *thanks, Mom, for believing in these weird words.*

About the Author

Lindsay Rae Brown lives with her husband and two children in Lethbridge, Alberta. When she's not toiling away at her day job in the laundry room, she writes and publishes humorous essays in various corners of the web. Her work has been showcased in periodicals such as The Dead Mule, The Maine Review, and Defenestration. You can find more of Lindsay's work on Medium.com (she's the one wearing a unicorn onesie in her profile pic—you can't miss her). Stay updated on Lindsay's upcoming work by connecting on Facebook or signing up for her Substack newsletter (It's Just Foam).

Manufactured by Amazon.ca
Bolton, ON

37817238R00132